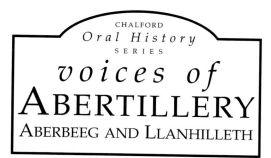

CHALFORD
Oral History
SERIES

voices of
ABERTILLERY
ABERBEEG AND LLANHILLETH

The remodelling of the road layout at Aberbeeg to remove a traffic bottleneck is well underway in this view from above the village, early 1980s.

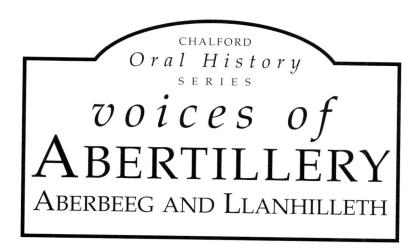

CHALFORD
Oral History
SERIES

voices of
ABERTILLERY
ABERBEEG AND LLANHILLETH

Compiled by
Simon Eckley and Don Bearcroft
in association with
Abertillery & District Museum Society
and the people of the valley

CHALFORD

First published 1996
Copyright © Simon Eckley, Don Bearcroft
and the interviewees of Abertillery, Aberbeeg and Llanhilleth, 1996

The Chalford Publishing Company
St Mary's Mill, Chalford,
Stroud, Gloucestershire, GL6 8NX

ISBN 0 7524 0696 5

Typesetting and origination by
The Chalford Publishing Company
Printed in Great Britain by
Redwood Books, Trowbridge

This book is dedicated to the founder members of the Abertillery & District Museum Society, the volunteers who have run it, but, most of all, to the people of our valley. This is their story.

Vivian Colliery officials at a dinner in Hereford. From left to right, back row: George Matthews (deputy), Idris Brickell (pitman), Evelyn Brickell (Ken's wife), Mrs Lewis, Mel Smith (timekeeper), Godfery Lewi (head timekeeper), Colin Rougton (storekeeper), Joe Hoskins (deputy), Ken Brickell (deputy), Le Selwyn (oveman), Ron Cummings (deputy), Merv Watkins (master haulier), Joe Langley (overman Gwyn Phillips (Coal Board negotiator), Trevor Evans (under manager), Cliff Lee (head electrician Harold Adams (fire officer), Mrs Lewis. Front row: Nellie Brickell, Jack Thomas (senior overman), M Thomas, Mrs Smith, Herbert Smith (deputy), Tom Wallace (manager), Mrs Evans (under manage wife), Mrs Adams.

Interior of E. Marenghi's Arcade Cafe, No 5 The Arcade, Abertillery, c. 1925. Mrs Doris Bearcroft worked here as a cook in the late 1920s.

CONTENTS

Bro. Levi Brooks, seen here with sash, chain collar, apron and gauntlets, was a member of the Newbridge Lodge (2063) of the Royal Order of Antediluvian Buffalo. He was the brother of Oliver Brooks, then the relieving officer for Abertillery, and the father of Ray Brooks of Princess Street. This picture was taken in 1933 shortly after he was 'exalted to the Third Degree Knighthood of Merit' in a ceremony which took place at the Station Hotel in Abertillery on 15 November. The exalting officer was Bro. S. Williams KOM, PPGP.

INTRODUCTION

Abertillery and District Museum Society was founded on 30 September 1964. The aim of the members was to establish and maintain a museum for and about the Abertillery area. Their efforts were successful and in 1972 Abertillery Museum was set up in the 'new' library on Oak Street, in a room specifically set aside for that purpose by Monmouthshire County Council.

One aspect of the society's work was to collect material and information concerning the past of our community. One method of gathering information, which shows how far-sighted the founder members were, was to tape-record interviews with the older inhabitants of the district and have them tell of their experiences during their lifetime and the changes in the district.

Some years before I became curator, these tapes in the museum were brought to my attention by our late treasurer, Mr Bill Selway. He allowed me to borrow them and on returning them I told him that they had made a big impression on me, doubly so as the two people who conducted the interviews – Mr Tom Philips (vice-president) and Mr Fred Gunter (treasurer) – had both taught me in school. While listening to the tapes it was as if I had been transported back in time to the classroom where they were giving a history lesson. It was then that Bill suggested that I should continue with these interviews.

My first interview was with Mrs Emily Newbold, aged over 90, who lived just behind the Institute. She was a grand old lady and had led an interesting life, having been a active

Abertillery boys' brigade, c. 1920.

member of both Abertillery Labour Party and the Aberbeeg Hospital League. The next recording was made with Mr Reg Hoskins of Queen Street. I knew Reg from my days as an electrician at Six Bells Colliery and he drove a haulage machine in the Vivian. He told me of his father's heroic death in a colliery accident, his life in the Boys' Brigade and his swimming achievements. These, like many other of the events and personalities recalled by our interviewees, are illustrated in the pages of our book by pictures taken straight from the family album or from a dusty, but carefully preserved, box.

One of the most interesting people I have interviewed has sadly since died: a reminder of how important it is to preserve the lifetime of experience that the older members of the community have before it is too late. Mr W. ('Billy') Hill had spent his life working in the collieries but also farming at Gilfach-wen and Ty Dafydd on Mynydd Llanhilleth. On being introduced to him at a barn in Cwm Nant-y-groes, he greeted me in

Welsh. It was a cold day with snow on the ground and in the air. The interview took place in the barn with the sheep chewing the hay in their stalls, and with us stood around a brazier. Billy seemed impervious to the cold but kept pushing me nearer the fire and calling me 'boy bach'. With him in his 90s and me in my 50s I suppose I was! I thought every minute of our conversation worthwhile. When we said goodbye he picked up a bale of hay and strolled off with his two dogs at his heels.

While we were working on *Abertillery, Aberbeeg and Llanhilleth* in the *Archive Photographs* series, my co-author Simon Eckley became aware of these tapes. He suggested that, together with photographs to illustrate them, they would make a good book. I replied, 'In about ten years time when I get over this one!' Well, in the end, together we have finished the book within two years. With the help of my 'long-suffering' wife, Peggy, several more interviews have been conducted, when time and my health allowed, and on occasions people kindly came to the house to be interviewed; Simon, meanwhile, has done the work of transcribing the tapes and compiling the text and pictures.

During the preparation of the first book I had talked to several interesting people who were first on my list to approach for an interview. Among them were Bob Fowler, who tells of driving an engine over Crumlin viaduct shortly before it was demolished; the late Ken Brickell, who helped us identify the only photograph of the isolation hospital I have ever seen; Mr George Morgan who tells of his father's life in the trenches during the First World War; George's wife, Irene, who tells of working as a maid in a house in the Royal Crescent, Bath – an upstairs and downstairs regime. Her interview for the job could have come out of the pages of a Dickensian novel.

To these individuals above and to the many others who have been involved in the production of this book, I am exceptionally grateful. It has been a rare privilege to be invited to share their memories and bring them to a wider audience.

This year has not been particularly kind either to myself or the museum. In the summer we suffered the tragic loss of Ralph Robinson, our chairman and a personal friend, and due to the expansion of Abertillery library we have been forced to seek a new home for the museum. However, the latter may prove a blessing in disguise, as we are now in the process of raising funds to create a purpose-built museum building in the town, with the aid of Lottery money and the support of Kath Davies of the Council of Museums in Wales; Frank Olding, our Curatorial Advisor; and Blaenau Gwent County Council

Property Services department. With their help the museum artefacts will be safely stored until the new building is ready. Until that time, the Museum Society will continue holding a full programme of lectures and field trips will-provide both an historical service for local schools and information resource for the general public.

Don Bearcroft
48 Princess Street, Abertillery

The memories contained within this book have been arranged according to major, over-arching themes such as The mines, Living through the Depression and Entertainment and sport. Each section contains extracts from interviews with several individuals, illustrated, where possible, and arranged under a succession of subject headings. Some of our interviewees wished to contribute anonymously but at the end of the majority of extracts the reader will find the initials of the source.

At the conclusion of the interviews I had hours and hours of recordings to digest and the process of transcribing the extracts has taken me many months. My principle aim when compiling the book was to let the interviewees tell the story of their community in their own words. I have tried to limit 'tidying up' of speech to a minimum and to preserve the rhythms and vocabulary used wherever possible. I hope the finished result makes for an enjoyable, but also thought-provoking, read and that a rounded impression is presented of what it was like to grow up, live and work in the area and what it means, today, to call it home.

Simon Eckley

CHAPTER 1
The mines

Miners' meeting at the bottom end of Abertillery Park during the 1921 Strike. Glandwr Street is clearly visible in the background.

A boy miner pictured at the pithead with his older butties.

It was near enough all pit work... there was the tinworks and that's about it, it was all pits and collieries. [RH]

Years and years ago, certain people had money and what did they do with it? They didn't keep it in the bank. No, they invested it and sunk a hole in the ground. If there wasn't any coal there they'd have lost their money but because there was coal there they had to employ people to get the coal out. That was us. Our capital was our hands; their capital was cash. Now, during the period that cash was coming in everything was alright but when it got tight instead of them [the capitalists] losing their cash the miners had to pay for it. That's the struggle.

From school straight into the mines

I remember Dad saying he was short when he started to work. He was about twelve and he went into work with his lamp, tripped over and his lamp went out. The next day he done it again and he had a good leathering off his father [Joe Horler] for doing it. He said he never let his lamp go out after that. [AH]

I went to Cwmtillery Colliery to work, no training, straight down the pit. I went up on the Friday and signed on, showed them my birth certificate and then on the Monday I walked with my father from Powell Street to Cwmtillery Colliery and went down the pit and I worked as a collier's helper. The first collier I worked with for two years and then he had an accident – a stone fell on his head and he had to finish work. Well, I had another man to work with then for quite a long while. My job was to fill the drams. We had the smaller drams in those days and we had what we used to call a 'racer' tram. We used to build him up on the sides to get as much in as possible and we used the larger coal for that. There was an art in that and that was my job as collier's helper. They got the drams from there by horse. A horse used to come in and bring us an empty one and take the full one out. [MM]

I left school when I was thirteen, that was roughly about the '20 mark. I wasn't old enough to go down the pit so I worked a twelve-month on the milk and then I went down the pit [the Gray Colliery] when I was fourteen. I was engine driving 'on the coffee pot'. We called them coffee pots because they were small engines. I worked in the Gray till that finished. Those pits were three – Penybont, Gray and Vivian. You could walk through to either of them. The only time I ever come up that pit [Penybont] was when we had a breakage on the winder. [RH]

I started work at fifteen and a half in Cwmtillery Colliery. I was a collier's helper and that meant using the curling box. If you were caught not using him you were threatened with the sack. You had to put the coal into the curling box with your hands to make sure there was no muck. It had to be clean. No way did they pay for small coal only for 'lump coal'. When I started to work it was 15s

4d before stoppages and 14s 8d after. It went to your butty and if you got a penny too much you had to buy chalk with it. The man you worked for paid you. He drew his pay at the office. I worked as a collier's helper. Then I think it was the Porter Award [c. 1944] which gave hauliers and other people a bob or so more so I went driving for about eleven years. The four ponies I broke in were Hitcher, Haggis, Golf and Gaffer. It was heading and stall when I started and we would take the coal to a double parting. I spent twenty years in Cwmtillery. That's when I passed to become a fireman. I didn't intend taking it actually... I done it for the family. [JB]

Dirty coal

You wasn't to use a shovel to fill the drams. You had to use what you call a curling box. You had to put the box down, put all the coal in and carry it and tip it in the dram. It was a monotonous job. If you were caught with dirty coal in the dram it would be turned out. Then either you was fined or you had to go on top of the pit for a day cleaning the coal. That was the penalty you had to pay if they found you with dirty coal. They would put your number by the pit cage and if that was there it meant that the next day you couldn't go down the pit and you had to go on the screens, on the muck belt picking the dirt out.

Wages in the pits

When I started in the pit my wages were under two pound, roughly about the 30 shilling mark or under that

The Gray Colliery, Abertillery, c. 1905.

I think. I remember working in the Vivian at £1 19s [c. 1922]. A married man doing the same job as me was having more. That was never right but that's what happened with the wages in them days. [RH]

Haulage of men underground

In the Vivian I drove all the big haulages and the same down Six. The manrider didn't come out until I went to Six Bells to take the men from there up to the Vivian. You had to be a bit more alert with men riding. If you went too fast it hit automatic brakes and so I always brought it down in gear so that I kept the same speed all the way. I never had no trouble. Later, they done away with the mine cars and had just ordinary drams. Then, they put a safety rope from the back right up to the front so the drams couldn't run away. Assuming there was twenty drams on the train there would perhaps be half a dozen shackles all the way up. [RH]

Soaked to the skin

I worked in this five-foot seam in Cwmtillery No 2 and then they closed the No 2 down and it was all in Cwmtillery No 1. Then, we had to go into the Garw seam which was anything from about 2ft to 2ft 10in and I can tell you the biggest worry of my life was on one occasion I was working in 1ft 10in and I couldn't even kneel. I was on my side and because of the conditions (the water would congregate in this swamp) I'd go in my dirty clothes but I'd take another set of dry clothes with me so that at the end of my shift I would take the wet off, put the dry on to come out, carry the wet out and take it to the boiler room up in the baths so that would dry then ready for next day.

It was so low and wet and because of the conditions instead of having eight yards of coal to get off I was allowed to have six. As soon as my coal was off I could come up the pit – you could either have water money or go out when you finished. About 1950 I was getting £9 20d a week for this. [HM]

My father [Will Harrhy] moved the levels over to the Llanhilleth side. When I started to work, a little boy of fourteen, they were putting an incline down opposite the Walpole. I don't think there was ever a dirtier job. Water was a problem and you had a hand-pump for this, a tall one with two handles on it. It was meant for two people really. I couldn't reach the handles, so I had to pull the bar. Now the valve used to leak a bit down below and if you pulled slow it used to squish the water up in your face. I can tell you that by eight o'clock in the morning I was wet through. You used to wring your pullover or your shirt and your feet were never dry. There were wellington boots but we were never allowed to have them because [as children] you couldn't get them small enough to fit us. So you had to put up with it. Lots of times I'd be stood up on this thing and I'd take my socks off letting my boots get wet. It didn't matter about them and when you come out you could put your socks on. [DH]

Rose Heyworth

When I went to Rose Heyworth in 1949, I would say there were about eight faces working at that time.

The old coal had run out by then and they were working the seams above the old coal. There was a yard seam at the north as you go up towards the South Griffin. It was only a yard high but it was good coal. There were two faces – A and G – one was working north and the other was working backwards south. I was a mason at Rose Heyworth and I spent thirty-five years altogether, twenty-three underground and the rest on top of the pit until damaging the vertebra in my neck running into a girder which I'd put up there in the first place! My biggest job was building ventilation doors underground and fitting all the roller wheels to guide the drams on the bends where the journeys used to go round. [JS]

A lot of rats and an evil fusty smell

The west had a higher seam, well nigh a five-foot seam. Because it had a very shaly, slaty top they used to leave a foot of the coal up to hold the roof and they worked underneath. It was a very hot district and nobody liked going in there. There were a lot of rats and an evil, fusty smell. If you could keep out of that district you kept out of it. But being a mason I had to go all over the pit... I had no choice. [JS]

Repairing work

I used to repair the shaft at Rose Heyworth where we had one main shaft. That was a downcast and it was very cold and wet. Before, they had a 'dandy' pit, 80 yards off the shaft, right down to the bottom of the old coal. They drove down this dandy shaft and they put the pit-bottom in first and then drove the main shaft down to it. That was long before my time, of course. There was an old haulier (Bryn Hayward from Bournville) and he used to say that he drove the bricks from the bottom of the dandy pit to the proper bottom of Rose Heyworth to help to build it. The archway there was about 26ft wide and 15ft high. It was a big arch and that went back for a good sixty or seventy yards from the pit-bottom. That was very big for them times. [JS]

Held for years with wooden wedges

We used to have the bond covered over in plastic sheeting. That was the only way you could keep dry. My job was to repair the brickwork and I had to get outside the bond to do that. If we knew we were going down, we'd go to the sawmill on top of the pit the day before and ask them to cut us oak or beech wedges, little wedges about four inches long tapering to nothing and about two or three inches wide. We'd have a pile of them cut in the saw and they used to have a shelf above the fire and they'd dry them all out for us. We'd take a bag of them with us down the pit and we'd wedge the bricks in. We couldn't put mortar in there as it wouldn't set. Rose Heyworth pit was held for years with wooden wedges! [JS]

Falling down the South Griffin shaft

The South Griffin was a terrible pit to work in and I near lost my life in there. One side of the pit was squeezing so much that they put skids around the side of the bond so that he would slide through like a sledge against the side of the shaft. Our side only had two guide ropes on and when you went down they used to catch in the brickwork and you would put your foot out and shove the bond back off the edge of the brickwork. The shaft wasn't straight, it was squeezing in and if the ropes started to sway a little bit the bond would swing over and catch in the brickwork. There was me, my brother Owen, my cousin Jack Patfield, and two others – Dick Evans and Jack Evans. We were all on the bond going down and the cage got caught on the side of the pit. It was swinging and as we was going down the rope was getting slack and the bottom started to topple over. It tilted right and we was all against the one side gate holding on. Then, all of a sudden, it broke away and fell and I remember Dick Evans wanting to get out. There was a block coming out of the brickwork across the other side of the shaft to carry things across like pipes and haulage ropes. It was a clamp for the piping system and he wanted to get out on that. 'Well', I said, 'the bond is safe now. It hasn't pulled the cap by the sound of it'. It was like a kid with a yo-yo, going up and down for a bit and they didn't wind us up for a good ten or twenty minutes when the winder noticed the slack coming down in front of him. He didn't know whether the bond was still on the end of the rope. We had this knocker in the pit. We carried an iron plate and we knocked it with a lump hammer, or whatever you had, two or three times whichever was descent or rise. We waited a bit and knocked and he didn't pull, but after a couple of times he moved it up. By the time we got up, the manager and the agent from Ebbw Vale was on top of the pit and Wilf Coleman persuaded us to go back down and we all went. 'If you don't go now,' he said, 'your nerves will go'. So we had a cigarette [Wilf Coleman had a pack of Players] and we sat for a good three-quarters of an hour I expect to have this cigarette and a talk. [JS]

Another close shave

I remember walking up on my own from the South Griffin across to 'G' in Rose Heyworth. We had a main and tail rope there and what you used to do was put your foot on the rope and see which way it was pulling. But I had misjudged him, it was the wrong rope. I had the tail, and the journey was coming towards me. I got up on the pipe on the side and the edges of the drams ripped all my clothes off my stomach. It was that close it frightened me to death. If it had been an old dram, with a big piece sticking out, he'd have gored my stomach! [JS]

No compensation

My grandfather was using the hatchet on some timber, it slipped and cut his hand. Of course, he felt he had to go to work to keep the money coming in for the family and so it turned to septicaemia and went up and killed him. He died when he was only 54. There was no compensation because he still went to work with the injury. I don't suppose he ever would have reported it. [HM]

Death of a hero

I worked in the Gray two years and in 1924 my father got killed there. I can remember that to this day. I was working in the same district. The gaffer haulier said, 'Come down the heading with me, I want you'. He took me down the heading and I didn't twig it. They took stretchers down then and after the stretcher gone by he brought me back up and got a chap to bring me home. 'Well Reg,' he said, 'You' father have had an accident'. I said, 'How bad?' 'Oh, I don't know', he said. I walked home in my working clothes [at that time there were no pit head baths] to tell my mother. I was on my way to tell my aunt in Gray Street when a lady came on to me at the Foundry Bridge. She said, 'Son, who's the man killed in the Gray pit?' 'Oh', I said, 'nobody that I know of, there's been an accident, though.' [RH]

Carnegie Award for heroism

He [Richard Hoskins] got killed saving lives. He knew all about that, of course. What had happened was this: a haulage rope broke and instead of him just getting on the side out of the way he run down to warn people at the heading. There was a couple of work-

15

The Six Bells Colliery before electrification.

men down there but the dram caught up with him and slam.... He had the Carnegie Award. This was not just for miners but for anyone saving lives. You had to be approved, you couldn't just put in and have it, you had to have it verified. Mother had a cheque every month and I can remember this was always about £6 odd. That was really good money in them days and, of course, she had the compensation for my father which was round about £350. That was a lot of money in them days and what I liked about that was when the compensation run out the Carnegie people made it back up. Every two years, the Lord Provost of Edinburgh came down to visit us and he always wanted to know how we were situated and whether we wanted anything. [RH]

Accident at the Gray

My father was originally a miner. He was brought home from the Gray pit one day when I was still in Bryngwyn School. I remember going home and someone waiting to meet me to tell me not to knock. There was straw spread out in front of the door to cut out the noise of the horses and carts. My father had a brain haemorrhage and collapsed in the pit. They'd brought him home and he was there for weeks and weeks. As a result he had to give up pit work and eventually he was able to get a job within the Ministry of Labour as a civil servant. And that's where he finished his working life. [WGH]

'For blood and coaldust when they link
Make hieroglyphs of Indian ink'

Like many other miners, my father had the experience of being buried while working underground. He told me that one time when he was working on the face the coal came over on him and he was completely buried. As the weight on him increased so the pain became less until he blacked out. He came to with the pain increasing and the weight on him becoming less as his rescuers dug him out. He received first-aid and came home where my mother picked the pieces of coal out of his scalp with a tweezers.

In later years when asked about the blue scars that covered his head he would tell his grandchildren, 'That's my own personal road map!' [DTB]

My father worked until he was 72. He had an accident in work; he was repairing a parting with his cap on the floor with the dog nails in. A stone cut his head and the wound would not heal. He had to go to the surgery every day to get it dressed but when the snow came they gave him pads to do it himself. He had a stroke then, although they said the accident had nothing to do with it. [KB]

The grey faces

I remember the grey faces – the men who worked in the pit and would come home coughing. That was one of the reasons I got out of the pit. [GM]

The dust

I never remember my father working because he had dust. He'd worked as a stoker in Aberbeeg Colliery [the old Aberbeeg Colliery at the bottom of the hill]. He came down this way when there was a shortage of work [in the West of England] and I think he was a Swindon man. I never remember him going to bed. He was always sat in the chair and when night come mother put another chair for him to put his legs up on and covered him up. He had this dust so bad that he couldn't get up the few stairs that we had in River Row. We used to eat well because all the boys were 'mortgaged' to Kibby's next door. They all worked for Kibby's because it kept the family budget. Our Bill drove the van, Jim used to go out on the van with old man Kibby and our John worked in the bakehouse. [BF]

Conscripted into the mines

I was supposed to report to Chesterfield but when it came to the crunch and I had to go, I thought, 'Oh, I'm not particular to go and fight'. So, I asked could I go into the mine and I had to go to an appeal court because they said, no, I couldn't. But having been to Cwmtillery pit and seen the manager he said, 'Look, we can get around that. Start work Monday and when you go to the appeal court you can say you're working in the mine'.

Four days into working in the mine I was with my uncle in a very shallow seam. It was 3ft high and I can remember there was what they called a shaker conveyor – it was modern for those days. One of the bolts came out and knocked the stick out and this huge rock came down and smashed my shovel and my lamp. I can remember shivering and shaking and my uncle putting his coat over me for the rest of the shift. When I came up, I said, 'I'm not going back, I want to go to the forces' and, of

Miners emerging from the cage at Cwmtillery, c. 1920.

course, they said, 'Well, you can't have it both ways!'

[The accident] shook me up so much that for three weeks I couldn't go to work. But then I went back with an uncle who was deputy there and I went into a seam that was five foot and I wasn't so bad then. [HM]

The pit doctor

I worked with Dr Gregory in Cwmtillery. He was the pit doctor. Our surgery was overlooking the co-op. The men were great. My mother came from Cwmtillery and when the doctor would say to men that had come, 'Oh, see the dispenser, Miss Wallace', they would say to me, 'Oh, you must be Nellie Combstock's daughter' because they knew that she had married Joe Wallace. A big day was when the men had to come to have their ears syringed. Now, this chap had an accident and he was all roughly bandaged up. Dr Gregory was helping me and we were very careful. We did stitching there as they didn't send them to the hospital

then. You did as much as you could to help the hospitals. Now, we had a dose of Salvolatile on the side because this man was definitely going to faint. But, as we undone the bandage, part of the thumb fell off and it was I who had the dose of salts! That was the only time in my life that I ever fainted. [MD]

Improvements in the safety of the mines

Whatever they say about nationalised industries the standards of safety improved a terrific lot. Because I wanted to earn as much money as I could, I took risks but when nationalisation come in, you couldn't take the risks. If you did you were really in for it! [HM]

Explosions

I went over to two explosions. I walked from Cwmtillery to Milfraen, Blaenavon. There was an explosion

Men leaving work at Six Bells Colliery, c. 1978.

there so I walked over to see that. I was only a young boy then and I can remember them bringing the dead men up in drams. You could see just their legs, as they brought them up, tarpaulin over them. And I also walked over to the Marine but I didn't go near the colliery... you weren't allowed to. [RH]

Six Bells, 28 June 1960

My father and his brothers came here to work from Salisbury. My mother (Charlotte Herbert) came from Treherbert and her father was killed sinking No 5 (Six Bells). The sides all collapsed when they were down there and buried them. A lot were killed sinking the pit. My mother said there would always be blood on the pit because of this. That was their belief in the olden days. [KB]

When they had the disaster I was on the day shift at Cwmtillery. I was on the pit-bottom, so one of our other bandsman, Clayton Powell had come down to say there'd been a terrible accident down Six Bells. I came up the pit and I had a Wolseley 4/44 so without having any dinner we went straight to the Salvation Army Hall. We boiled an urn of water, made the tea, and took it down in the boot of the 4/44. We were there right on the spot. The Army was the first people there and I can remember, I think it was Whitehead the NUM president, said, while other organisations are going through the procedure of organising things, the Army's there. We were there all day giving out cups of tea. That was a very harrowing thing. [HM]

19

I was in No 4 pit at Six Bells at the time of the explosion. I did not know anything until I went to work in the afternoon. At first, I was making the gangs up, then I went with the electrical engineers and electricians down 5 to turn the power off both pits about 7 p.m. As we were going down to the pit head there were a lot of Salvation Army people about. One lady shook my hand and said, 'Be careful, my son. There's enough of your comrades down there now.' That was it – I was as full as a damned egg then.

Well, we went down 5 and while we were down there the canary we had went quiet. One of the boys was tapping on the cage, 'Are you dead, canary?' He was alright, though, he just didn't like working double shifts! What they do with the canary is that they pump oxygen and this goes under the wing. The canary breathes much quicker than a man and when he's suffering he puts his head under his wing so he can get extra oxygen. If you spotted the canary doing that, it was time to get out. [KB]

My brother-in-law [Roy Edwards] was killed up there. He was working down O 20 in the tailroad. Twenty-eight he was. We used to talk about the gas in Six Bells and Roy used to say, 'Oh, I can run, I'm a good runner.' My wife woke me up about 10-11 o'clock this Tuesday morning (I'd been working nights). She said, 'There's been an explosion in Six Bells, go and see if Roy's alright!' When I got there I saw the boys and they said he's still down there and it's gone. So I called my mother and then went up and told my sister. The following day Tom Brom [Tom Bromwich] and me went to identi-fy him. That was a terrible day. They were all lined up in the tram shop. He wasn't hurt at all, not a mark on him. Just caught the gas. You just wanted to shake him and wake him up. [BSH]

Telling the management what they want to hear

As an official I tried to be fair. Being Salvation Army I couldn't tell a lie and so my answers to the management weren't the answers they wanted. We were at loggerheads at times. I can remember on one particular occasion a deputy got me on the tannoy to come down to his district to help. When I went in all the roof had collapsed. I said, 'What has happened here?' He said, 'Nothing'. I said, 'What do you mean, it's shut-in?' 'No,' he said, 'When we get out, I'm saying on my report: Rubbish cleared, two rings need to be erected.'

When we got up the pit he went in front of the manager and told him this. I was there with him and the manager asked me if I had anything to report and I said, 'The roof at the tipping end during the night has come down from twelve to only eight inches'. [The manager replied,] 'Oh, you're always a Jonah. I never hear anything good from you. It's about time I had something good from you.'

So, when they went in and found this other place where it was shut-in nothing was said. I would have been far better off if I'd said it was the same as it was last night! [HM]

Among those pictured at the bar in Llanhilleth Institute are Billy 'Shilling' (Chairman), E. Dennis, Clive Davies, Mel Minchin, Jimmy Smith, R. Taylor, B. Morris, George Smith, C. Price (Steward).

Us against them

I was a packer, then I became captain of a team of about 30 or 35 and then I went on the union as representative. I had to make sure that the money was right for each boy. You dealt with the overman to see how many yards you had to do. You could cheat your way a bit and they [the management] would be going mad. They'd make a mark with a ring and say now this is the mark we got to go from next time. Well we'd go and pull it out and put it down below and get extras. Sometimes, they come to a road and they'd paid for 150 yards and there was only a hundred yards done and then the manager was screaming and shouting. They was good days in the pit... I'd go back tomorrow. When all the pits were going you knew everyone and there was a friendly atmosphere. [BSH]

I never liked pit work but there WAS something, you can't define it, something special with the men. You could have a blazing row with a man but if anything was wrong you'd help each other. It was a marvellous thing. [HM]

Deputies

The deputy came from your side but when they got on the other side some of them looked down on you. They was terrible, mun. There was a saying that if you wasn't a good work-men they made you a fireman. The lazier you were the better you had a chance of a job as an official. You give the working-class man power and he's the worst of the lot. Some were differ-ent. For example, Ken Brickell was very fair, a good boss. He was a man's man. What he had to say he told you. [BSH]

Retirement

I felt sick for this one chap, Jack Challenger [who retired from Llanhilleth Colliery in the 1960s]. Now that man had worked in the pit for fifty-odd years and the clerk came in to the manager and said, 'Mr Challenger's out here, he's finishing and he wants his cheque,' and the manager said, 'Bring him in!'. 'All the best then, so long' – that was it. That's how cold it was. They didn't even give him a drink or have a collection to buy him a cup or some-thing. [BSH]

Closure

'Lan' closed in March 1969. I never thought they'd close that pit, we were doing well down there. We were losing tuppence ha'penny a ton but we'd made a million and a half the year before. We was too militant. It was a family pit. If one man was sent out we'd all go out... it was that kind of pit. Yet Six Bells was no different. That was another family pit. If someone was killed and buried you knew who it was. They were good boys there. I expect

about 150 of us went up from 'Lan' to Six Bells and the reception was great from the boys there. I don't think we were organised enough to keep it open. About six hundred were working in 'Lan' when it closed. A lot of them fin-ished and they got nothing... they were treated terrible. If you didn't want to go to another pit you went straight on the dole and there was no redundancy pay-ment. [BSH]

The small mineowner

My father always termed himself as a small mines owner – a colliery proprietor. The first he had were up Brynithel on the Cemetery Road. He had four levels up there and as much as 42 men working for him. He called them the New Argoed levels. They had an incline coming down by where the mortuary is now because the lorries he had then was only a small ton lorry (a Ford) and they used to have Sentinel lorries run by steam and it held about eight or ten tons of coal and they used to put a couple of hundredweight of coal to feed the boiler in the front. The man who owned these was a man by the name of Tim Price. He used to fetch a lot of the coal. Generally it was horse and cart [carrying half a ton at a time] but we had a lorry. [DH]

£100 paid the wages of forty men

On the Friday I had to go down to Bakers the coal-merchant's in Six Bells with the bill for the coal that they had bought, probably about £50 and £50 then, mind [c. 1932]. I was told to keep my hand in my pocket and hold the money tight. Well, you were afraid to look left and right with all this money. Also, on a Friday, I had to go to the bank – I was only about ten or eleven – and fetch £100. I had to have 60 pound-notes, 30 ten-shilling notes and the rest had to be in change: half-crowns, two-shilling pieces, shillings and pennies. That £100 would pay forty men's wages. The labourer used to get £2 8s; the collier £2 12s 6d and the timberman £2 10s. Then, there used to be a few labourers outside pushing drams and general factotums having about thirty shillings a week each, which was twelve shillings more than the dole then. [DH]

Working the levels

We were working a combination of both long-wall and heading and stall. You had two seams of coal. The one had been worked from about 1812 to 1852. But they could only work the coal so far because they'd have trouble with the air, with water and with jumps. But because we had fans and pumps we were able to work this coal – the Mynyddislwyn seam. In them days you had to make a thing pay. There was so much competition that the price of coal was so low that you couldn't afford to do it tidy. You couldn't follow good mining practice. You had to try and work so much coal to pay for what you were doing. One of the things was you had to have returns. Every so often you had to make a return because in front of you there was a big jump, perhaps as much as fifteen feet down. [DH]

Picking coal and the ghosts of old miners

In the '21 and the '26 Strikes, men used to go up the hillsides to get their coal. It was so near to the surface that it wasn't much trouble to move this bit of grass and gravel. It wasn't a very good coal, though, it was the outcrop. Well, some of these men went in and they never had no timber, half of them. Some used to put up little sticks and once or twice they used to get buried up there. They put all these little levels in and used to fill their bags and drag them down over the mountain. Well, we'd heard the story that in the '21 Strike there was an Irishman by the name of Durban. [He was trapped in a fall] and they was never able to get him out. He was left there.

Now, we had to go near or underneath this work because we were working the Bottom Coal – the bottom part of the two Mynyddislwyn seams. Of course, they would never work that because it was too thin. It was two foot six and then there was four feet of clay and then this top seam which was four feet to four feet six thick. That was what the '21 strikers were working. They had the crop out of that. No big firm would touch that because that was like the safeguard, or the coal wasn't no good. It used to burn very very fast; it wouldn't make much ash, mind, but it wouldn't last very long.

We were coming near to where this supposed Durban was buried underneath and we was about thirty yards from coming out at the surface. We thought we'd go round the other side and get our surveyors to give us a point but in the

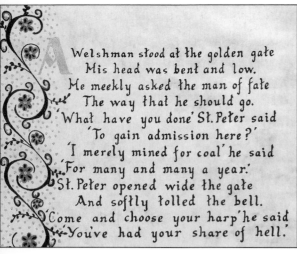

A Welshman stood at the golden gate
His head was bent and low.
He meekly asked the man of fate
The way that he should go.
'What have you done' St. Peter said
'To gain admission here?'
'I merely mined for coal' he said
'For many and many a year.'
St. Peter opened wide the gate
And softly tolled the bell.
'Come and choose your harp' he said
'You've had your share of hell.'

This verse has hung for many years on the walls of the 'Stute' in Llanhilleth.

process of coming out we met a lot of strange things happening. We used to see lights and hear a lot of knocking that used to come like the old miners. And there was nobody else working within half of mile of us. As regards to the lights it may have been the reflection of our lamps in the water ahead and there is also a type of timber, a kind of a French larch, which if you take the bark off the phosphate in it do glimmer. So we always put these things down to that. But then things began to happen which made you take notice and a couple of times it was so queer that some of the men wouldn't work in there. So, to try to disprove it, one day we turned all the machinery off, all the compressors, all the generators and the level was dead still.

We had to pull out these pumps out of the water to check if there was enough of oil in them. You filled these bottles of oil up to the top because they had to last a week. Now, I was doing this job and I went to go back to get some more oil from where there was a 40-gallon barrel on the side. As I was turning around I saw another light besides my own. No, I thought, it was a reflection in the water. I went now and done the job and screwed the caps up and then after you go half-way up you think to yourself, 'Now, did I screw them up tight?' So, lots of times you went back to check and it was coming back down that I noticed this light again. I turned my own light off but left the dimmer on and still the light was bright and it was moving. I sat on the side and waited but the light was there and it was moving back and fore. I was more than a bit scared. I went out and got my brother and we went back in. That's when we heard the tapping again and this time it was quicker like an emergency tapping the same as before but faster. [DH]

CHAPTER 2

Living through the Depression

Stoning the blacklegs

I lived up Pantypwdyn when I was a girl and I can remember the time when the men were on strike. Opposite the Vivian there's a bank by what used to be the Drill Hall and the women used to stand on there throwing stones at the blacklegs as they were being taken home from the pit. This one day things got so bad that 'Super of Police' Baker on a white horse (opposite where Wilson's Garage is now) read the Riot Act and that meant everyone had to disperse. The blacklegs used to come from the Gray, walking down through Church Street. There would be a police cordon either side of them. They used to go up the back way on Alexandra Road sometimes but people would still be waiting for them by the Vivian pit as they came out there. When they did come across the bottom here, people used to throw everything they could find at them. [DB]

Isolation during the General Strike

In the General Strike [4-12 May 1926] there was no connections with anyone. They used to have bulletins sent from one area to another and if you pinned that bulletin on your front door the police would come and rip it off. One man used to travel back and fore on somebody's motor-bike and he'd get to know how that area was progressing with the strike. Then, he'd pin it on the door and the people around here would know. But, if the police had seen him do it they would have arrested him and ripped it off. The only way of connecting with people was on the quiet.

In the 1926 Strike the Salvation Army band travelled all over the country raising money for the boot fund to buy boots for the children of the unemployed. Ray Veal was the main cornet player They did one tour of the West of England down as far as Plymouth and one all though Wales and when he came back his lips had split right open from the effort of playing concerts every day. [HM]

The relief man

Even when they had a relieving effort in the '26 Strike, my mother would insist on paying it all back. They gave us money and I can tell you how tight it was. I was schooling then and our main meal was lunch... rice with currants on the one day and Quaker oats on the other. I still say it was a wonderful life. We had the relief fund through the council. The relieving officer was a chap called John Phillips and then Oliver Brooks [Ray Brooks' father] done it after. [JB]

One of the inspectors was a cousin to my mother, Ivor Griffiths. We used to have a song: 'We'll hang Ivor Griffiths on the sour apple tree'. They didn't like him, but he had to do his job, of course. They came around in 1926 bringing the relief to people's doors. 'Here's the relief man coming!' My mother had sixteen shillings a week, twelve for the woman and four for the child. Nothing for the men, of course, because they were on strike. [MH]

Community spirit

There was more of a community spirit because when they were out of work everybody was in the same boat. It was chiefly the pits, but today it isn't, of course. There's so many working and others not working and it's awful really when they haven't had the chance. But years ago when the pits were out, well, everybody was out. You'd see them waiting to sign on for their dole. There'd be a queue down by where the Cottonwood Café [the old post office] was. [MH]

Picking coal from the tips

My earliest memory is picking coal from Six Bells pit in the '21 Strike with my father. I was about five. We seen a policeman and it frightened me to death. We were taking the coal to burn in the house, we didn't sell any. [JB]

The women used to pick coal in 1921. The trucks would be tipping down and afterwards people would go and get tiny lumps. In the holidays, the kids would go and pick some and that would keep us amused and out of mischief. But, it was dangerous sometimes, people wouldn't wait till the trucks had emptied. When they were tipping it down, they'd be waiting to get bigger lumps. [MH]

Stealing from filled trams

The Alwyn level went right up to Cwmtillery. It was a very long level

26

with six horses and I started work there as a collier's helper. In the depression, eight or ten people were caught up there stealing coal in the night. Six policemen went in and caught them. The next morning the tram of coal was taken to court as evidence! All our tools were left out but they stole the coal we had cut ourselves so we didn't have any sympathy for them. If they'd cut their own coal we wouldn't have minded, but they stole out of the trams. [KB]

The ash man

I remember one time, there was a little boy very ill up where we lived, by the chapel. They had sawdust on the roads because of the heavy old carts, so as not to disturb the little child. Every day the ash man would come around; there was so much ash when the pits were going and everybody with coal fires. You'd be shaking this old coconut matting and you'd get covered in dust yourself. You didn't have to shake them after eight o'clock in the morning – that was a law brought out by the council. [MH]

Death in the lakes

Those lakes [up in Cwmtillery] can tell some tales. During the 1921 Strike there was a family. The man was Italian but I think he'd been here for donkey's years and his son was born here. They [the administrators of poor relief for Monmouthshire] wouldn't give him any help, I think. He tried to earn some money making ice-cream and he had a trolley thing taking it round. But that poor chap ended up in the pond. A decent family, too, it was awful. They lived up in Woodland Terrace.

It was so hot that year [1921] that they started swimming in the pond and one poor fellow he got tangled with the weeds and got drowned. Then another time, in the winter, children were sliding on the ice coming home from church and one fell in. The others made a chain with their arms to try and rescue him but he drowned. Quite a number of people were drowned up there and the same up Penyfan. [MH]

Making ends meet

Well, when we were unemployed Mam used to go out and clean, paper a house through for half a crown Mam would. I can remember coming home to tea [in the 1930s] to a large bowl of beetroot and thinking it was wonderful – we'd have bread and beetroot for tea. We never went without food, we weren't hungry, but you couldn't say it was fancy. [AH]

Bryngwyn feeding centre

The feeding centre was up on the side of Bryngwyn Road, just below Bryngwyn School and my grandfather worked in there. So, we used to go all rushing in there every day for our dinner and there'd be long tables. I'd always be after my grandfather to have a ha'penny off him so I could buy sweets when I came out. Mr Rogers was the one who was in charge there (Bill Rogers' father). The staff all wore big white aprons and there were big boilers. [AH]

VISIT OF HIS MAJESTY THE KING

TO

GLEBE SPORTS GROUND, ABERTILLERY,

Thursday, November 19th, 1936,
at 1.40 p.m.

Admit _____ Mrs A M Jenkins _____

You are requested to present this Ticket not later than 1.15 p.m.

J. DOWNS, Honorary Secretary.

A ticket to see the King in Abertillery, 1936.

Abertillery men line up to be presented to King Edward VIII, 1936.

Mother's sacrifice

I remember going to the feeding centre in Rhiw Parc and this was round about the time that Edward VIII the uncrowned king came to Abertillery. Looking back now, I'm sure we used to have bread and a thin smearing of 'marg' and the jam always felt like as if it was sawdust; it didn't taste like jam. I'd come home, and mother would ask me what I'd had to eat and I'd say. I didn't think about it at the time but I remember she used to sacrifice and give me a little bit more because I wasn't full. You'd put the tea in the pot and then later on you would dry that tea and try and make another cup with it. [HM]

The boot fund

What I do remember of those days is the boot fund. The town had a boot fund and schoolchildren were entitled to a new pair of boots or shoes every so often. But you had to go to your headmaster and show him your boots to prove that you needed a new pair. Of course, in those days very few people could afford to have shoes repaired so they were worn until the soles were almost gone. I remember Edgar Lloyd taking me one day (I'd had to go to ask for boots) and he didn't have a pair to fit me. But, having looked at my boots, he took me to the other end of the school where the girls' cloakrooms were and found a pair of high-legged girl's boots which fitted and he took me back to his room and cut the tops off with a scissors so that I had what appeared to be a pair of boy's boots. [WGH]

From hand to mouth

When the men had to work on, I remember going down to the coke ovens to get the pay off my father. For one thing, they didn't want to lose it, another thing we'd be waiting for it. He used to get paid on a Saturday when I was little and we had to scramble off to shop at the last minute. Then, it come that he was paid on a Friday, which was better. The Bon Marché would be packed on a Saturday night. Even if you only wanted a pair of socks or the slightest thing you'd have to wait and wait and wait. In the week people didn't have any money to go, you see, but on a Friday night when the men had had their pay they'd be rushing to the co-op [in Cwmtillery] to shop and over Gwern Berthi there was a co-operative (Blaenau Gwent had one and, of course, down town). [MH]

The lowest of the low

My family was the lowest of the low. There was nobody poorer than us. My father was on basic down the bottom of the line and we didn't have a lot of money in the household with seven boys and three girls. If you wanted to go to the pictures down Crumlin, you'd get a carrier bag of coal up and sell it for sixpence or a shilling. That's what we used to do as there was nothing given to you in them days. My father suffered with dermatitis and lost a lot of work because of that and he liked his couple of pints. He was a wonderful father, but he was hard, and he lived hard. We had bread and butter, bread and jam, bread and dripping. But we used to go rabbit-

The newly-built Abertillery Guild Hall, 1930s.

ing and we'd catch rabbits. We always had a joint on a Sunday. It was survival but everyone had it bad in those days. [BSH]

Getting work in the Depression

I was fourteen when I left school. When the *Gazette* used to come people'd be looking for a job. They'd didn't have much hopes though. But I remember my sister got a job from looking in the *Gazette* it was working in Thomas' China Shop in Church Street. She had 7/6 a week, a big deal – Bon Marché only got paid five and people thought they were the cat's whiskers to work there because they were dressed in their black dresses. Talk about slave labour. [MH]

Abertillery Guild Hall

Mam and Dad were members of Tabernacle and Mr Isaacs [the minister, who eventually went to a church in Weston] was the instigator of getting this hall built in Castle Street. This was the Guild Hall – built to give people who were unemployed something to do. It was a lovely hall; there was small rooms at the back facing the colliery but the front part was a big hall and they had work-rooms there. You could do carpentry and they started a ladies' guild there for needlework and knitting and tapestry. My mother went there for years and years. I've got some beautiful cloths here Mam done... there was also a reading room. There are still big rose bushes growing there that they planted... there's no garden now, but every year they do grow. Concerts and keep fit classes, folk dancing, everything was going on down there. [AH]

MINISTRY OF FOOD

LICENCE No. R.L. 289.
S. Wa. 7.

LICENCE TO SELL FOODSTUFFS BY RETAIL

THE FOOD CONTROL COMMITTEE FOR THE DISTRICT OF

HEREBY LICENSES

Abertillery Town Guild.

AS A RETAIL DEALER IN THE FOLLOWING FOODS
IN RESPECT OF THE BUSINESS CARRIED ON AT

Castle Street, Abertillery, Mon.

BACON AND HAM, UNCOOKED.	FLOUR.	MILK, FRESH.
BACON AND HAM, COOKED.	FRUIT, BOTTLED OR CANNED.	MILK, CANNED.
BISCUITS, RUSKS AND CRISP-BREADS.	FRUIT, CRYSTALLISED.	MILK, DRIED.
BLANCMANGE POWDER.	FRUIT CURDS.	MINCEMEAT.
CORNFLOUR AND CUSTARD POWDER.	FRUIT, DRIED OR EVAPORATED.	NUTS.
BREAD.	FRUIT, FRESH.	OATMEAL AND OATFLAKES.
BUTTER.	GAME.	PICKLES AND SAUCES.
CAKES.	HONEY.	POTATOES.
CANNED BEANS.	JAM AND MARMALADE.	POULTRY (INCLUDING TURKEYS).
CEREAL BREAKFAST FOODS.	LARD AND COMPOUND LARD.	RABBITS.
CHEESE (INCLUDING PROCESSED CHEESE).	MACARONI, SPAGHETTI, AND VERMICELLI.	RICE AND EDIBLE RICE PRODUCTS.
CHOCOLATE AND SUGAR CONFECTIONERY.	MARGARINE.	SAGO AND TAPIOCA.
COCOA.	MEAT, CHILLED, FRESH OR FROZEN.	SAUSAGES.
COFFEE.		SEMOLINA.
COFFEE ESSENCE (INCLUDING COFFEE & CHICORY ESSENCE).	MEAT, CANNED OR PRESERVED OTHER THAN CANNED CORNED BEEF, CANNED CORNED MUTTON AND CANNED CORNED PORK.	SOUPS, CANNED OR DESICCATED.
EDIBLE AND COOKING FATS.	MEAT, COOKED.	SOYA FLOUR.
EDIBLE EGG PRODUCTS.	MEAT PASTES.	SUGAR.
EGGS.	MEAT PASTRIES (INCLUDING SAUSAGE ROLLS).	SYRUP AND TREACLE.
FISH, WET.	MEAT PIES.	TABLE JELLIES.
FISH, CURED AND DRIED.		TEA.
FISH, IN CANS, GLASSES OR OTHER AIR TIGHT CONTAINERS.	MEAT PRODUCTS, MANUFACTURED OR CANNED MEAT, NOT IN AIR-TIGHT CONTAINERS.	VEGETABLES, FRESH, OTHER THAN POTATOES.
FISH PASTES.	MEAT ROLL OR GALANTINES, CANNED.	VEGETABLES, BOTTLED OR CANNED, OTHER THAN CANNED BEANS.
		VEGETABLES, DRIED.

FOOD OFFICE STAMP

SIGNED ON BEHALF OF THE FOOD CONTROL COMMITTEE

SIGNATURE..................

At its hall, Abertillery Town Guild was licensed to sell only the goods not crossed out above.

31

Wrapped in cotton wool

I was a premature baby, three pound odd. After I was born they wrapped me up and put me on the bed and said, 'Don't think too much of him, Mrs Mason, I'm afraid he's not going to live'. For months after that, they had me in a little shoe box in the fireplace, wrapped in cotton wool which was soaked in olive oil, to survive. I haven't done so bad, I've just got up to seventy-one. [HM]

Bathtime

There is something to be said for large families but on bath night it must have been a nightmare for Mam. The fire was made up soon after tea and a huge saucepan and kettle were put on to get hot for the first bath. Whoever got bathed first was lucky, because he or she got hot dry towels and Mam's undivided attention. But, often, just when the second one was put in the tin bath in front of the fire, Dad would call out from the shop which we then run in the small front room. 'Gwen, could you come here a minute.' Well, Mam would go in but, instead of a minute, time passed and when she came out to continue bathing us the water would be almost cold from the draught at the back door. We would be shivering and this together with the rest of us arguing with each other used to reduce her to tears and every week she used to threaten she would jump in the river. This always had the desired effect and for a while there would be total silence. Then, when we were all clean and ready for bed Mam would hand us our supper which consisted of half a round of bread covered in lard or dripping with salt on it and a glass of water. [EW]

I heard my father say that when he and his two brothers were working in Cwmtillery pit, you used to bath at home. If they all come up at the same time, they would all run different ways to try to get home so they did have the clean water for the bath. Very often, there was a terrible scum on the water for the third one! [HM]

Celluloid ducks and wooden engines

The Salvation Army band had gone away to Tottenham. I was having a bath in front of the fire in this little tin bath and my father had brought back some celluloid ducks. I can remember putting them in the bath and floating them and to me that was a wonderful present. My main Christmas present one year was when my father had brought a block home from work; he had sawn off the timbers, scraped off the bark, painted it red and green and put some wooden wheels on it. It was supposed to be a GWR [Great Western Railway] train and I thought that was marvellous at the time because we didn't have anything else. Nuts, an orange and apple would be in the stocking and then our main present would be something like that wooden engine. [HM]

Cwmtillery in the 1930s

My father worked in the washery. To see it now, you'd never believe it. There would be the coke ovens at the washery and, oh! it was lovely on a winter's night, it seemed to warm you up. Then the flames from Ebbw Vale steelworks would be leaping over the mountain from the next valley and when it was so cold it used to be lovely to see that walking up Crook Hill. We were only two children and my sister had started working then. She was working for a relative who kept a wallpaper shop in town. For women, it was either in service and for the men, the pit. Talk about the great exodus in the thirties that went away to work. A lot never come back and settled away. I started work in a house at the bottom of Alma Street in one of those villas – 23 shillings a month. I was only sixteen and I was doing the housekeeping and cooking. [MH]

Diaspora from the valleys

My mother had eleven sisters altogether. The biggest part of them moved away during the bad times, up to places like Croydon and were put into service. They married London people, Cockneys as we call them. I got more cousins in London than in South Wales as far as I know. [JS]

Poverty: loss of the breadwinner

My father worked in the pit in Llanhilleth. He was a fireman but he had a severe stroke when he was 40 and the right side and the speech were lost. We were four children and the youngest was three. You couldn't go to the post office with a book in those days. There was nothing. We hadn't saved very much but the bit we had saved was used up, and my mother sold all her jewellery, her rings and broaches to keep us. We survived, but we went without. My father had nothing from the colliery not even coal and that was Mam's bitterest thing – coal was expensive.

Mam and I we had to wash my father and dress him but he was a wonderful man, he really was. He fought all the time. For thirty-odd years he was trying to speak. We could understand him after a while, and he was able to go back and fore across the road. He was a marvellous man who fought hard. What my mother had to put up with I don't care to think.

She was a teacher before she was married but when she got married that was it, of course. [When Dad was ill she went back to work] and she taught in Llanhilleth Old School and, for a short time, in Abertillery teaching English and music, and evening classes. When I was growing up, there wasn't any money so I went down to Foster James, the manager of the Home and Colonial, and he offered me a job. I'd been to Newbridge Grammar School and passed.

Then one day Mum said, 'You'll have to do more than this. Now will you be a teacher?' This was the last thing I wanted. I'm an out-of-doors girl, very much so. But 'yes, alright Mam'. I started over at the Old School as an 'uncertif' as they called them in those days – an uncertificated teacher. Then, an order came from 'the powers that be' that you had to have your certificate or you'd be put off and, of course, Mam said, 'They can't put you off, you're the breadwinner.' (The other three children were much younger). It was against the grain for my Mam to go to see a councillor, but she must have gone and spoken to somebody and said, 'It can't be. You can't put this girl off'. Mam had her certificate. Now, for her days that was exceptional and because she was a certificated teacher they put her on for two years for me to got to college [Swansea Training College]. Now, where was the money to come from? Well, £5 came from the Abertillery Council, £100 from Newport County Council – a loan not a grant – and it was paid back when I started teaching. I kept all those receipts and every penny was paid back at 30 shillings a month. It took six years.

So, of course, when I was teaching we weren't rich but life was easier. I loved the children; I had little ones up to the age of seven but mostly the reception class – the first class – and I really did love them. When I finished up at Soffryd I was teaching the grandchildren of the ones I had first taught nearly forty years before.

I'd do anything for a sarsaparilla

I remember having a row off my father. He used to buy chocolate. A half-pound block of Cadburys was eight pence ha'penny and you had to get this from a shop down the bottom of Alma Street called Terrot's shop. The woman there was a widow and she had a son called Bill, who used to play the banjo and I had to go there to patronise them. But when Smith's [W.H. Smith] in town

opened, they had it cheaper at a cut-price – seven pence ha'penny – but with a stick-on label on it. They also had jars of sarsaparilla in Terrot's and for a ha'penny you could have a glass of this sarsaparilla. So, you'd buy a block of chocolate for seven pence ha'penny, and try and take the label off, so you could have the ha'penny then for a glass of sarsaparilla, with still a ha'penny left over for a couple of aniseed balls! But there was always a piece of the blessed thing that was stuck. You used to use your finger to wet it and try and get it off. You'd come home and see if you could get away with it but you couldn't. First of all, you were a bit longer as you had to go into town and second there was this mark you couldn't get off. So, I lost out! [DH]

The toughest of starts to life

My mother died when I was very young, just over four. She had a bad heart but I didn't know. I can remember catching hold of her hand and walking up Newall Street and then she'd stop, then we'd go a few more yards, stop – she couldn't do it because of her heart. I had no brothers and sisters, there was only me as she was too ill, always. I always remember her as being ill. When she died, I was brought up with my grandmother.

My father worked in the Gray pit. After the 1926 Strike he never worked again. It wasn't only the depression, because the day before they got married he had an accident in the pit to his eye. He had to go to Bristol to have that seen to and he wore those tiny weeny glasses, terrible. They lived in Tillery

Abertillery Linen League, c. 1925.

Street [initially] and then my mother was so ill when she was pregnant with me they had to move up to No 2 Newall Street and I was born there. [RM]

Better healthcare

In 1921, Marie Stopes (1880-1958), the British birth-control campaigner, had opened the first birth-control clinic in Britain – in Holloway, London. Four years later there were plans to set one up in Aberbeeg.

A man by the name of Dai Dagger (the brother of George Dagger MP) got in touch with Marie Stopes and persuaded her to come and open a clinic in Aberbeeg. So, Marie Stopes then employed a nurse and this nurse ran a clinic in the hospital [1925]. At that time birth control was taboo. Well this nurse was so disheartened with the number of people that did come that it fell through because of lack of support.

The Gwent Gazette records the verbal slanging match between supporters and opponents of the birth control clinic through 1925 An exasperated editor was finally induced to publish a note to say that everything that could be said about the matter had been said.

Beatrice Green

Beatrice Green (née Dykes) was a great worker in the town. She was a schoolteacher and very involved in the church life. Also, she was secretary of the Linen League for the hospital and she was responsible for raising money. Apparently, she was a very good speaker and they said [in her obituary in the newspaper] she certainly would have gone into Parliament because she had a brilliant brain. She'd gone to Russia on a deputation with the Labour Party and she'd picked up some kind of bug, come back and died in Aberbeeg. And as a result of that, because of the work that she did, the people and, I think, the Linen League raised money and they bought an ambulance. George Pile was the driver of what became 'Beatrice 1' and when that had served its purpose they bought another one and named it 'Beatrice 2'. So that was done in recognition of her great service to the hospital. She was only in her thirties and she left two young boys. [KD]

A mile of pennies for the hospital

I was a member of the Labour Party for 50 years [1920-1970 with certificate of merit signed by Jeffrey Thomas MP] and I collected money for our hospital. I used to go round the houses on a Friday afternoon to collect pennies. I was vice-chairman of the League of Friends at the hospital. I remember John Snellgrove cut the first sod for the hospital. It was Aberbeeg Miners Hospital. The men used to put some after, out of their pay packet [a penny in the pound] but the women collected pennies first. The people used to put the pennies on the pavement in rows. I had a mile of pennies stretching down Church Street and up Somerset Street to the Bon Marché and George Dagger [MP for Abertillery, 1929-50] gave half a crown. In the

street where I lived, where the swimming baths were, there was a room built there and the Linen League used to go in there to cut bandages ready for the hospital: Mrs Seabourne and Mrs Holman and Mrs Atty and all those big bugs was in there. [EN]

The fever hospital

My father was taken there years ago before I was born. He had a fever and he was in there for about six weeks altogether and my mother wasn't allowed to visit. She used to take my sister and go and sit up on the mountainside for him to look through the window to see them. [AH]

The only way to Green Meadow Farm was up Crook Hill and then from there by a road to the farm, all the rest was fields. The other road was to the fever hospital where my sister worked as a cleaner. The road was from Rock Street and only the old ambulance (Beatrice) could use it. The gates were

Staff at the isolation hospital, 1920s.

kept locked and the driver had to get the keys from where they were kept at Mason's (who had the shoe shop in town) – the big house at the end of Rock Street. [KB]

When we were children we always used to play in Gray Street because it was flat and the ball wouldn't run down the hill. We were always known as the Gray Street gang. Years ago, going back to the twenties, there used to be a rut over the other side of the road which the pit horses and the dray horses used to wear away. That was where you fetched your horse manure, there was always plenty of it and flies. Something I always remember is that someone would shout, 'Fever!' and an old black wagon with a red cross on the side would be coming up here – George Patfield was the driver. It was people going up to the isolation hospital. You could see the kids crying through the window because they were all covered in smallpox. Well, we'd run like hell away right down Gray Street to get out of the way because we was always told, 'Don't go near that cart or you'll catch it! You'll be like those'. So when someone shouted 'Fever!' it was like someone shouting 'Look out, there's a bomb coming!' The cart would go up to Adam Street across Rock Street and then they had a winding path all the way up to the hospital. [KJ]

Large families and lost children

There were the awful times when Mama had a still-born child. All these things seemed to happen when we were lying like sardines three to a bed. I can still remember Mama moaning and crying and lots of hurried footsteps on the landing. No-one came in to explain anything and we all held our breath knowing something terrible was happening. We began to cry and only then Mrs Homer, our lovely neighbour from next-door, popped her head around the door to tell us all to be good, 'Be quiet, your mama is ill and the doctor is taking her to hospital.' We never knew just how many babies there would have been but eventually we ended up a family of ten. [EW]

Making ends meet: faggots and peas

Mam started to make and sell faggots and peas to supplement the housekeeping. So Thursday night would find her in the pantry, the mincer clamped to the shelf with piles of liver, lights, beef pieces, onions, bread – a backbreaking job with a small mincer and all this after a hard day's work. Then the faggots had to be made: all the ingredients were lifted into a large brown earthenware vessel. Everything was mixed up well and then the seasoning and herbs were added. The faggots were fashioned between Mam's hands, each one seeming to be exactly the same size as the rest. This done, they were laid together in large roasting tins and covered in water and put into the oven to be cooked ready for heating up next day. The smells which soon filled our kitchen were wonderful and it got to be quite exciting when, next day, the passage started to fill up with people coming to buy their hot faggots and peas.

From this small effort, Dad decided to give up work at the level and open a shop in our front-room. We kept everything from sweets and brushes to 'Carter's pink pills for pale people'.

After school each day, we had to walk the mile or so from Aberbeeg School to Commercial Road, Llanhilleth to the Baptist church and the hated feeding centre. This was where we ate every day with some of the hundreds of children whose parents just couldn't afford to feed them. Dinner every day was mincemeat in thin gravy and potatoes and tea was bread dipped in watered jam. I can still see the red stain of it as it spread to every corner of the bread. The head of the feeding centre was a Mr Richards who was fat, jovial and plump; he walked with a heavy limp so we thought he had a wooden leg. Mr Richards had very soft spot for my sister Ann and liked to show it by giving here little extras on the side, like butter on her bread or a piece of cake. [EW]

'I can't afford to keep you in shoes!'

I never knew what wellingtons felt like until I was about twelve. We were desperately poor and we used to go to school with pieces of cardboard in our shoes to cover the holes. But in the summer, there was the thrill of wading through the water down Old Woodland Terrace because it used to rush in the gutter down there. Your feet was hot and the water was cold and it was the most marvellous feeling!

It was so wonderful to have new shoes but money was so tight that Mam used to say, 'Don't show them off in front of your father,' because he'd say, 'Bloody shoes again!' If you said you were going out to play 'scotch it would be: 'You're not bloody kicking those shoes, I can't afford to keep you in shoes'. So you had to nearly hide your feet when you had new shoes on. [EW]

Hand-me-down clothes

All our clothes were hand-me-downs, often from the Williams family, who to us were like gentry because Trevor had the barber's shop in Aberbeeg and Jack and the others were schoolteachers and they were all very well-educated. When I was fourteen, Mrs Williams gave me this lovely coat. It was gorgeous, with a lovely leather belt; I was quite tall and I could have carried it off. I took it home and I said to Mam, 'Look what Mrs Williams has given me,' and my father said to me, 'Lil's going to service next week, she needs that more than you.' Of course, because she was little, it was nearly down to her feet but that didn't matter because she had a good coat. [EW]

Carol singing for sweets

We didn't have the money for sweets. We had a ha'penny every Friday and we had to spend it in our own shop. We never had the ha'penny in our hand so we used to look for the biggest thing which was usually a lucky bag. Lou Poole used to have a shop in the square [at Aberbeeg]. Well, he was a little old man, a bachelor, and it was a magic shop, it kept everything. At

Christmas, when we went out carol singing – and we really did go carol singing, we'd give 'em their money's worth – we'd end up with a couple of shillings and we'd come back to Uncle Lou's. It was always well-lit up and there was a place for you to sit outside. We'd take out all this money and we'd share it out and get a 2oz bar of chocolate for Mam and two ounces for Dad. [EW]

Treating all the boys

This one day Dad went in to buy a box of woodbines – he usually sent me – and Uncle Lou said to him, 'I think I'd better tell you Charlie. One of your boys has been spending rather a lot of money here.' Now, we never had any money to spend. We had 'cut out' apples out of the shop and a ha'penny on Fridays. 'What do you mean, Lou?'. 'Well, he's been in here treating all the boys in Aberbeeg.' Dad couldn't wait to get back. He got hold of Colin and he said, 'I hear you've come into money, my son.' 'What do you mean, Dad?' 'Oh, I hear you've been treating all the boys in Uncle Lou's'. By this time Colin was getting very worried. 'How did you come by this money, my son? 'Running errands, Dad', Colin said and Dad gave him a smack across the ear. 'You must have run your bloody legs off!'

He'd taken ten shillings [from the till in the shop]. Well, in those days, it was impossible to spend ten shillings and you 'could' have treated the whole of Aberbeeg! 'So, what have you done with the rest of it?' and Colin had to take my father to the corner as you turn from Aberbeeg into New Woodland Terrace. There was a wall there and he pulled out a stone and there was the change. [EW]

Dad's sweet shop and temptation

Mam was out one day, when I was back home with this shadow on my lung. Dad said, 'I think your father'll have a bath, bach. You sit in the shop.' So, I sat on a pop box in the shop and I was watching all these chocolates and sweets. We were brought up so strict that we never did take anything. But I thought I've got to have something so I took a Turkish delight. They weren't in wrappers in those days, it used to be in a little tray. I spent so long wondering about whether to take this thing that I'd only taken one bite when Dad opened the middle door, 'I've finished now, bach' and I had a mouthful of Turkish delight. He said, 'Good God, the first of my children I can't trust'. I nearly died and I didn't know what to do with the rest of it. I just cleared out of the door and I didn't go back for hours.

He used to put the cheap things in the front of the window and the dear things at the back. Well, the 'PKs' were always in the front and one day we did take the catch off the window and took a PK. Well, of course, you was chew chew chew spit, chew chew chew spit. We couldn't let anyone smell our breath and we couldn't be seen to be chewing. So, we had no joy out of it at all. It doesn't pay to steal I can tell you!

Colin got caught on a Sunday morning. We used to have chamber pots under the bed in those days and Dad heard him on the landing: 'Where are you going, my son?' 'Down to the lav, Dad.' But we only used to go to the lav at certain times of the day; it was unheard of to go early in the morning. So, Colin went down and he was rather a long time coming back and Dad was wise. He got out of bed and on the landing sure enough he saw Colin with a handful and a mouthful of chocolate dragees (little tiny ovals they were a favourite with everybody) and he copped it that day.

I remember that we used to have 'tobacco' – long thin pieces of coconut covered in sweet cocoa – and we used to sell Tizer. If Dad had old apples he wanted to sell he'd give them a new name and say these are 'apples special' and he'd give them a name you'd never heard of in your life! [EW]

Sunday, the best day, if there wasn't seed cake!

Sunday was the best day of the week – that was the only time we had enough to eat. There were two plates on our table at tea-time: one was like a cabbage leaf and that held bread and butter and that was just for Dad and Mam and then there was another plate with margarine which was for us. And there was always a tin of fruit and cream or custard or whatever was going on Sunday and there was always a new cake. But on the days there was a seed cake I used to break my heart because I hated seed cake and there were so many seeds in it that by the time you'd pulled all them out you only had a couple of crumbs to eat! So, for me Sunday tea time was dodgy. If there was fruit cake I loved it, if there was seed cake I hated it. [EW]

Fried fish for Dad, toe rag for the kids

Until we were fourteen we never tasted butter. Because it was always Dad first. I suppose it was the way of those days. He'd say, 'Another cup of tea, Gwen' but although the teapot was just behind him, he'd never dream of getting up and getting it. He was waited on hand and foot. On Friday, when Mam went shopping in Fatty Barter's, who used to keep the fish shop in Aberbeeg, and she'd get a lovely piece of fried fish for Dad. We'd never tasted it in our lives, but in those days as today the batter stuck to the paper so as Mam took the fish off we'd scramble for the paper to scrape off the batter. You can't imagine it, can you? And he'd say, 'You sit on the stairs now and watch the shop while your mother and me have our tea'. We used to be counting the minutes because we'd be starving to think he was in there eating a piece of fish with batter on. We'd have bread and jam I expect. Sunday morning breakfasts was 'toe rag' as we used to call it – dried salt fish bought on a Saturday. It was like a bit of cardboard and came in great big pieces, two-foot long I expect. You soaked it overnight in cold water and it was very cheap but very good for you. On the Sunday morning, you'd boil it and you'd have a nice piece of that. But it was very sticky and I used to annoy Mam and Dad to death because I was the joker of the family and my fingers used to be stuck together with the glue from this fish. I used to open my fingers one by one and I had a clip on the side of the ear for doing it. [EW]

CHAPTER 3

Other work

A major local employer after the mines was traditionally the transport sector, particularly the railways. This unusual view was taken from one of the marvels of South Wales railway engineering – the Crumlin viaduct – and shows two competing forms of transport (rail and road) sweeping northwards. The Navigation Colliery can to seen to the left of picture, c. 1960.

Herbert Turner, yard master at Aberbeeg, 1920s.

'You'll never get on the railway, my boy!'

I started on the railway down at the loco shed. It was a career and a step up from the milk round. In those days it was either you went in the pit as a young boy or you'd try to get on the railway.

I can always remember when we were in Brynhyfryd School, we used to have to have a special train, one coach for all of us from Aberbeeg to go down to Llanhilleth. Now, before this one coach come in, the ordinary Newport passenger train used to be at the platform. Well, we got in the habit of hanging on the running boards when 'he' pulled out, until we thought, 'Well, it's going

fast enough for me to get off' and we'd run and jump off then. I got caught one day with the porter and he took me across to the station-master. Oh, aye, Old Alvie sat behind his desk pointing his finger and he said, 'You've jeopardised your chances of ever getting on the railway, my boy.' There's many a time I wished to God he'd kept his word! [BF]

Starting on the railway

I started at Aberbeeg loco shed as a cleaner boy in 1943. We used to clean engines until about half past one/two o'clock and then the charge-man used to give you a list. There was three calls – Llanhilleth, Brynithel and Aberbeeg – and he'd give you this list with the names of all the drivers and firemen and what time they had to be called. We used to have a driver, Stan Davies, who lived right opposite Jones' garage and then you'd have perhaps half an hour to get from there to Charlie Boucher's in Cwm Nant. You didn't have transport, it was all foot, no lights, only a little oil-lamp [nights]. We had a boy start one night and he said, 'How do I manage for a light?' and we said, 'Oh, you take one of those lamps up there'. But instead of him taking the little paraffin lamp, he took a ruddy great engine head-lamp and we didn't know until he came back in the early hours of the morning and he said, 'I ain't taking one of them lamps again, they ain't half heavy!' And he'd carried this engine lamp all round.

They always called Brynithel 'Little Swindon' because so many drivers, fireman and guards all lived up there. When I started on the railway prior to

Pontypool engine sheds with its facility for turning an engine.

that if you were in the loco sheds you had to live within a mile and an half radius so you could walk and get there for any shift. We used to have one bloke who walked from Blaenau Gwent Rows every day (Bryn Lawrence). [BF]

Sent to London to work

I went on to Oak Common. We didn't have no option, Aberbeeg was under the GWR. Where they wanted you, they sent you. In latter years, things altered and you could make an application to go where you wanted. But in our days as firemen we had to go where they wanted us. I was made a fireman for Oak Common up in London so away I had to go. We were only young firemen and the majority of the work was pulling the empty coaches up into

Paddington and bringing the returned trains back to sheds for cleaning and whathaveyou. I went up there in '44 and in '45, just as the war finished, I come back to Aberbeeg as a fireman and started in the junior links. [BF]

Bankers, goods and passengers

It always went in seniority on the railway. The junior hands had the junior work and so you went up through until you got up to the passenger trains. Well, at Aberbeeg, we started off on the small engines, on the bankers. Then, the next link was what we called the '42 link', that was a big goods engine, and then you ended up on the passenger link. We had the Glascoed line then, up the back from Llanhilleth. That was the only passenger train that used to go up that line.

43

It was a mineral line.

You'd be on the bankers waiting down here at Aberbeeg and when the trains come up from Newport up the valley he'd be a single load to Aberbeeg but from Aberbeeg to Ebbw Vale the gradient was steeper and we'd have to push 'em through, bank 'em through. We always used to come on the back end of the train and push them up to Ebbw Vale and then leave 'em and come back ready for the next one. When I went on the goods the majority of the work was when a load would fall down and loading empty mineral wagons back up anywhere and everywhere. We used to bring up 48 empties. I don't know what the load was going down. We'd have 24 iron ore and then you'd have a banker at Aberbeeg because that was well over the load for Ebbw Vale.

When I went up then on the passengers, I fired for a bloke by the name of Herbert Parry – a proper old worrier! I always had a good pal in the stores, a fellow by the name of Frank Bevan and when you got the engine ready in the morning you went to the stores and you drew out a bucket of tools as we called it: that was spanners, hand-brush, driver's feeders and a pet-pipe. That was the pipe to water the coal and keep it all clean. I had my own bucket of tools in the end. I kept all the spanners nice and clean and if it was possible to keep it Frank Bevan always kept me informed because every other bloke was after Fowler's bucket. With half of them if you wanted a spanner you put your hand in about two inches of oil and water to pick the spanner out.[BF]

The right tools for a fry up

This one morning old Frank Bevan gave me a brand-new shovel. When I was out on the footplate this fella from up the Garage (Stan Davies) said, 'What's that you got there?' I said, 'A new shovel.' 'Well,' he said, 'you can get rid of that.' 'What do you mean, get rid of that? I've just had it off Frank!' 'You get another one!' he said, 'an old one'. 'What's the matter with it?' 'Well, I've got to fry up and I'm not having that paint.' Well, of course, the paint hadn't burnt off and I had to get another shovel especially for him to fry his breakfast. Normally the shovel was like a frying pan, cleaner I expect because of the coal sliding on and off all the time. We used to use the shovel to wash our hands as well, of course. You'd tilt the shovel and make a little well in the back end of it and that would be to wash hands in. 'Put some water in there, mate, so I can wash my hands.' [BF]

Tricks at work

We used to have one bloke and he was easily persuaded. You could kid him along without any bother. There was two at Aberbeeg that were noted for 'hard hitting'. The one, Marshall Hopkins, he'd be awkward: if he thought you had a box full of fire he'd hardly open the regulator, if he thought you had your fire down on the baths he'd hit hell out of that engine and make you work like a devil to get a bit of fire in there for him. Now the boys persuaded this Sid Vaggs that Marshall had left Crumlin with a passenger and he'd put a spark up over the

44

Aberbeeg railwaymen, c. 1950. From left to right: Ron Woodward, Bob Fowler, Roy Boucher, Graham Jeffries, Mike Dennis.

viaduct. A couple of days after Vaggs said, 'He's a bloody liar 'cos I've tried and I can't do it.' You can just imagine him trying! [BF]

Basil Sanders

He used to carry everything to work in his box including his ruddy cheese ration. He said, 'They'll only eat it at home if I leave it there!' He came to work one morning and said, 'I bloody had 'em this morning. I put the wireless on loud [this was about three o'clock in the morning], come out and slammed the front door. Well, they don't think about me when I got to get up early in the morning. They got this record blaring out. So I've had my own back this morning. [BF]

Aberbeeg depot

It was a good depot, it was home from home down there. Good mates to work with. If you wanted anything done for you, you could always find somebody that would do it. [BF]

Railway line in Cwmtillery

The line used to go up from the Foundry Bridge or from the station right up to Cwmtillery. And there used to be an old engine down here. Where the football field is now, this big old engine would be puffing up and taking trucks to be filled at Cwmtillery colliery. They seemed to be alive in comparison to diesel. [MH]

View south from Crumlin Viaduct, c. 1960. A coal train is captured in full flight.

Crumlin Low Level station with a train crossing the viaduct above.

Aberbeeg station

In the winter it was always quite exciting to me to be waiting on the platform at Aberbeeg station. The train would come in under the bridge, with the road going over the top, and the place would be filled with smoke and steam as the engine pushed through. There were the old gas lamps on the station casting a pale yellow glow. You could hardly see the person next to you when the train pulled in. Of course, there was a big railway depot at Aberbeeg and it was a very busy junction. There was always quite a lot going on. [RR]

Crumlin Viaduct

We went across the viaduct with a light tender engine going to Aberdare one day, just a light engine, no trucks. It was frightening – you were so high up and at night-time you could feel him shaking. It was getting old and they made him single track. 'God there's Crumlin down there'. I never brought any passengers over. They used to have passengers from Pontypool going to the Vale of Neath and Swansea. It was five mile an hour going over the viaduct, they would knock the speed right down. There was a weight limit as well. [BF]

The thrill of the first cars

There wasn't all that much traffic about then. I can remember seeing the first streamlined cars with the sloping back and running up from Woodland Terrace up onto the road going up by the Methodist church (the Prims) in Aberbeeg because someone shouted that there was one going up there. That was the very latest. If we had half a chance, we used to like having a ride because all the cars then had a running board on the side. From the front wing they swept along the side and you could stand there and hold onto the window. So if we knew someone, we could have a little ride. [RR]

Give us a shove!

It was a quite common sight to see people pushing a car. The electrics weren't as good as they are now, the batteries weren't as good or they weren't charged. Quite often, on a frosty morning you'd be called upon to give a shove with a car to get it going. I remember after the war, when you had petrol, you had to carry a pint or two of oil especially if you were going any distance. The engines then used a lot of oil. For example, when my dad used to visit his brother in Gloucester, he always carried a pint of oil to top it up. [RR]

A car as our playhouse

I remember the first car they [Percy and Albert Williams of Princess Street] had was blue and black – a blue body with some black on it. And only two could sit in the front and the back was outside the car. You lifted the top up and you sat in there and sometimes they'd take us children for a ride around Abertillery. Of course, if it was raining you'd get wet. After that, they had another car, it was like a big limousine. That was green and black. When it came then that they wanted to get rid of

that car my father suggested that he would have it at the bottom of our garden. So, Reg Hoskins and the boys and my father and a few of them lifted the car up over from the back into the bottom of the garden. My father was going to have it as a workshed but it ended up as a playhouse for us children. And it would be nothing for about a dozen children to be in the back garden having picnics in the old car! My sister put curtains up and little shelves. We kept the back seat of the car but everything else was taken out and it was quite a large room. We had great fun in there. [AH]

Working for the council

I started work with Abertillery [Urban District] Council in 1932. Not long before that the staff had suffered a 10 per cent reduction in wages because of the economic situation. I started on the magnificent salary of ten shillings a week, out of which I paid, I think it was a penny a week to the hospital and thruppence a week for a doctor. [WGH]

Abertillery Tin Works

Percy Davies and Cliff Boots were friends of my father (Bill Dykes). They were boys in the tin works. You can tell by their dress that they worked in the mills. They wore little short aprons and protected their boots with strips of old 'belting' because the floor was hot and shiny. During the rolling process they threw the hot tin-plate across the floor.

The length of the tongs was impor-

Cliff Boots, Percy Davies and Bill Dykes, mill workers at Abertillery Tin Works, c. 1922.

tant and Dad would go to the blacksmith Mr Daniels, or his striker Ossie Pearce, and ask them to cut perhaps a quarter of an inch off the handle of the tongs. You would wonder why but it was crucial for the balance. Dad had furrows in his hands from using the hot tongs.

There was a family atmosphere in the tin works. They were very proud men and worked hard. The Robins were a large tin works family and they used to say that you had to be a 'Robin' to work there.

Jack Monger (Dad's uncle) was a shearer. He was the 'union man' and administered the Medical Aid Fund.

Dad spent 35 years in tin works leaving within twelve months of the works closing in the early 1950s. He could remember the rollers wearing bowler

hats to distinguish them from the rest of the work-force. Dad worked as a doubler for a number of years with Aubrey Morgan. Apparently, they had the record for rolling the highest number of boxes (98) on the Big Mill.

During the years of the Depression, whereas most people were completely out of work, the tin works would work sufficient time to complete any orders. When business picked up again they reopened the mills and Dad became a rollerman working on the electric mill. I believe that there were seven mills (four steam and three electric. Cyril Jones (furnaceman), George Tetley (doubler), Arthur Rees (ketcher) and the Pembridge brothers (first and second helpers) worked as a team with Dad as rollerman. [KD]

Warwill's Foundry

He [Ron Howells] worked in Warwill's Foundry. He was a moulder and worked up in Church Street; he was one of the first to move down when they bought where the tin works was. I can remember Mr Rees who owned the tin works. They used to make all those great big wheels for the top of the pits.

They were all like brothers really, they would all help one another. If anyone needed help, they'd be there to help one another. Ron was working there when he died. It was nothing for Ron, when we were courting, to work from about eight in the morning till ten in the night because the war was on. They worked hard down there. It was seven years before he was a moulder, he had to take an apprenticeship in it. Later, he was a foreman down there. [AH]

Jobs for everyone

When we came out of school [late 1940s] there were loads of jobs for everyone. The boys went into the pits and there were apprenticeships. They used to advertise for boys and girls to go into the shops and things like that. My eldest sister went to work in the Bon Marché. She was on commission and for every pound of goods she sold she used to get a farthing and I can remember because my sister was never good at adding up and she used have it every three months she'd come home and we'd be adding up these farthings religiously to work out how much commission she was going to have. I expect she was earning about 15 shillings a week. [JL]

Holman's Newsagent

I went to work at Holman's about '41/42. Stan Holman was in the Army then and Mrs Holman (Muriel) was there, she was nice. I was paid 6 shillings a week when I started. I had two shillings for my pocket money so Mam was keeping the other four shillings. When I left I think I was paid about 12 shillings.

I'd go in early, about seven, and do all the papers up for the round boys. Mrs Holman snr she used to live in the back of the shop. She was one of the old school, very straight-laced, very 'just so'. Ebenezer people they were. Mrs Holman and Stan Holman lived just at the start of Gladstone Street with her mother and father, Mr and Mrs Griffiths. Mr Griffiths worked in the Coal Board offices up in Cwmtillery. Blaenau Gwent people.

We used to have all the business people in the town come in for their newspapers and Mr Rees who owned the tin works used to come in every morning for his newspaper, chauffeur-driven. Oh, he was immaculately dressed and he was a nice man. What he was like in work I don't know but he was a gentleman. Gunn the solicitor he used to come in for his newspaper immaculately dressed. He used to wear grey spats. All the bank people used to come there for their papers and cigarettes and anything they wanted. [AH]

Tricky's shop

'Perc' used to keep a small shop next door to the Old Tyleryans Club and they used to have a back room where the men who were unemployed could go and sit and talk and make a cup of tea. Then, in the small front part was where he sold sweets. Dad used to take me in and I used to have Cadbury's chocolate drops by the two ounces or one ounces. [AH]

It was just like a little shop. Young lads would go in there and they would sell pop and the boys would just sit around and chat in a little back room where they sold a few sweets and ice-cream and things like that. Men used to go in to talk about sport because they were interested in all forms of sport. I can remember 'Perc' telling me that they had paid £80 to have this shop and the goodwill. I would say that was sometime in the twenties. I remember him telling me that they could buy six large bottles of pop for about 1/6 and they would sell glasses of this pop to lads who used to go in. There was never any trouble. 'Alb' and 'Perc' were perfect gentlemen and they never had any nonsense in the shop at all. If anyone started a quarrel they were out. In later years he had a slot machine, you could put pennies in it and balls would go around. On Sunday nights most of the girls used to walk around, they used to call it 'monkey parading'. A lot of the boys would come out of this shop and meet their girlfriends there. [JL]

He had to have his piece of bread

When I left school at fifteen, I done a milk round for a very short while because I started on the railway when I was sixteen. I worked for Bruton from Penyfan Isaf Farm, all horse and

S.G. Holman, newsagents and tobacconist, High Street, Abertillery.

cart work, and I used to deliver all the way down to Christchurch and Woodland Terrace, up to Warm Turn down as far as Ty Graig. The horse knew every call and there were some calls, for example Mrs Bungy in Woodland Terrace that he'd never go by without a piece of bread. You could do what you liked but he wouldn't go past there until he'd had his piece of bread! [BF]

The Princess Street diary

My father had two grocery shops and a dairy business. This house was one of the shops and the other was in

Horse and cart belonging to Kibby's bakery, Aberbeeg, 1920s.

Somerset Street and the dairy business was operated from here. He delivered all up round Rose Heyworth (there were no new houses then obviously) and all down Six Bells and Abertillery. He used a horse and cart. My uncle also had a dairy business. He lived in Six Bells and as far as I remember he had the car and they shared it. My father never drove it though. The shop would be open until nine or ten at night.

Farmers collecting spent grain from Webbs

On certain days Webbs brewery actually made the beer. When this was completed there were a lot of spent grains of barley, hops and so on which was waste as far as the brewing process was concerned. These were shovelled out and the local farmers would come with their carts and buy, well I presumed they gave something for it, a load of this. They used this to feed the pigs on the farms. I can well remember seeing a line of carts waiting for the brew to finish so they could collect the spent grain. Sometimes, it would be tipping down with rain and I can see the farmers now with an old felt hat pulled tightly down around their ears, an old mac or coat on and over their shoulders a heavy hop sack. They'd be sat there patiently as though the sun was shining. [RR]

The job of a brewery rep

Eventually a vacancy came for a rep's job, a traveller's job, which I kept for about twelve years altogether. Everybody thought it was the easiest job

Presentation to W.J. Jones, manager of Webbs Brewery, Aberbeeg.

in the world to sell beer but it was one of the hardest – you were up against so much competition. You had all the others – Symonds, Ansells, Mitchells, umpteen breweries. Of course, the reps only go round 'free trade' [freehouses] that's only clubs. I had the Eastern Valley, Newport, Cardiff area which they don't do these days as it's too big. Most of my business was Eastern Valley - Blaenavon, Pontypool, Cwmbran and mostly in Newport. The funniest part for any rep in those days was when visiting a small town such as Blaenavon where you had seven or eight clubs, maybe more, the old boys would be following you around from one club to another to get a free drink and some of them would be in their carpet slippers. They'd know the rep was in the area. You'd see them in the one club and then fifteen minutes later they'd be in the another club. I remember one old lady in one club; she used to have Guinness and the steward said to me one day, 'Well, she's had two and she don't have any more than two'. So, I

went to speak to her and said to her, 'Will you have a glass of Guinness, love?' and she said to me, 'Can I have the money instead to put in the 'diddler'?'

Working in the solicitor's

My grandmother thought I was right up the top of the social ladder [laughs]. Dear, dear, her granddaughter actually going to work for a solicitor and not going into a shop. When I started there I was earning £1 2s 6d and out of that I had to pay a stamp which was 2/3 and I used to give my mother half for my board and lodging. She'd have ten shillings and I'd have the ten shilling odd and if I wanted anything my father would lend me £5 and then I would have to give it him back every week and our Dad used to write it all down. He had a book and I used to say to him, 'Well don't you trust me, Dad?' And he used to say, 'You know where I am, my girl, and I know exactly where you are.'

53

£5 was a lot of money in those days and I'd go and buy a dress and a pair of shoes. You could buy it all with this £5 and I would pay him so much back each week and as it came down he would give me this £5 again and that went on until right after I was married. But, by the time I got married, he'd lend me £25. Our Dad never had any money – I suppose his capital was only £60 altogether – but it seemed a lot of money in those days. [JL]

Going to court

I used to have to go to court. I always had to wear a hat and me being a prim and proper miss I always made sure that I had a file in my hands so that no-one thought I was going in [for trial]. I would rush down to the bottom straight away to where all the solicitors were sitting. We used to deal with the local authority and one of my jobs was to issue the summonses for the people not paying rates. I used to have to go up in the witness box and take my oath to swear that I had actually prepared these summonses and I had posted them off. [JL]

The new Foundry Bridge

When I first started they were just bringing in the development to get rid of the old iron Foundry Bridge and the council then had to buy up a lot of houses on the end of Alma Street and at the top of Church Street. Beyond where the post office is now, there was a café and a butcher's shop and that had to come down so that the bridge could sweep around. I think about eight houses came down at the bottom of Alma Street to make way for this new bridge. There was a lot of work involved when the bridge was put up. It was one of the first of its type in this country and a type of construction that was certainly new to the area. [JL]

Travelling salesman

When we'd be coming out of school, there'd be the oilman coming with paraffin. We had paraffin lamps not gas and that was a new house we were living in. This old cart coming along with the paraffin would have all sorts on it. You could buy little potty wooden chairs for the kids, mats and rubbing boards. What he didn't have on his cart!

In the afternoon it would be the baker coming up Crook Hill and he would be covered in mud and that cart would be coming with bread and cakes. We used to hang on to it and have a ride.

The rag and bone man was always out. Where they ever got any rags from I don't know because people had to wear their clothes till they were dropping off. They even gave us kids things to eat. [AH]

Of course, we had lots of carts coming round selling things [in Aberbeeg]. There were greengrocers and Davies the oilman who used to sell paraffin and various things, hardware. Many items were sold on the road. The ice-cream vendor was a common sight on a tricycle with a big box and a churn packed with ice around it We'd have a

Kibby's shop, River Row, Aberbeeg, 1920s.

wafer or a cornet and sometimes we'd take a cup out and have a scoop in a cup. [RR]

The cockle man

My father was a cockle man. He used to keep his horse up at Penyfan Pond and when I was about nine or ten I used to have to walk up there to catch the horse and bring it down, harness him up for dad because he was working nights and he'd go out selling cockles. He done rag and boning as well. [BSH]

Hop-picking

It was a tradition to go up to hop-fields. From the end of August to the end of September, we'd be up there for five or six weeks. It was our annual holi-day. We went to a place called Ledbury in Herefordshire. It was nice there. You could pinch 'taters and eggs and if you got caught you had a hammering. If you didn't, you was a good boy! [BSH]

Pontlottyn v Bon Marché

When I went to live with my aunt they had one daughter who was working in the grocers over the far end of Somerset Street but another two worked in Pontlottyn. That was like Harrods in those days. But there was a snag: if you went to work there you had to work two years on apprenticeship learning how to serve a customer and you didn't get any money, no perks, nothing. That was wicked to my mind. I heard my dad say that my aunt was so proud and so pleased that her daughters worked there that she practically starved herself to keep them there. Bon Marché

Abertillery Co-op, with probably all its stock on display, 1940s.

was common. Pontlottyn was very posh. Pontlottyn looked down on Bon Marché. There was no thought of a union not in those days and they worked long hours early in the morning and they didn't close till six, even seven, weekdays and at the weekends they stayed open until eight or nine at night. They sold haberdashery, all the very best, silk stockings, very posh in those days and the dearest clothes and hats. Oh hats in those days were very ornamental. My cousin had one once [she worked at Pontlottyn] and she wore it to chapel this Sunday. I was with here and we were walking home and there was a few young lads and they started singing 'Horsey, keep your tail up' because she had two big feathers up in the front. She was so embarrassed, she never wore it again. [RM]

Rees' Golden Crust Bakery

I went to work there and I was supposed to be an apprentice to learn the trade. My wage was 10 shillings a week and it was 9 shillings and tuppence after stoppages. I started at eight o'clock and finished at five. Occasionally, when we had heavy snow, I used to have to go out and help on the van delivering bread to people's houses and sometimes I would go up to the top bakehouse where they bread was being baked and help out there. Mainly I was on the day shift in the bottom bakery.

The sugar used to come in bags and when they were emptied they cut up the cloth bag and I used to have a cloth apron made out of this bag. My job was greasing the tins, doing all the dirty work, washing up and all the rest of it and I wasn't learning a great deal.

Because the flour and damp would get on the floor you couldn't sweep because the floor was all concrete. We used to have a scraper with a sharp end on it and we used this to scrape and then sweep it up after. A lot of the men went to the forces and a man by the name of Phillips from Six Bells who was 65 and myself were the only two males there, all the rest were females.

We were working in the confectionery department and my whole job every day for 15 months was doing rock cakes, scones and what they called raspberry buns – I used to have to mix that with hands not a machine. These were sent down to the Golden Crust shop that used to be in Somerset Street and people would be queuing up to get these

because you couldn't get things like that. So, I developed and got better in the skills of the baking and I enjoyed it. I was making and decorating wedding cakes, in fact, I decorated my own wedding cake! This elderly gentleman, who had been in the trade all his life, he showed me how to do the piping. Of course, by the time I was getting a little bit proficient at it I was called up and I had to go into the mine. I was deferred from the February to the December as Rees's had asked for me to stay with them longer.

When the war ended Rees' asked me to go back to work there but the money I was getting there wasn't as good as the money I was getting in the mine because I had become a collier and I was

Work at Rees' Bakery, Abertillery, 1950s.

Supervising the bread oven at Rees' Bakery, 1950s.

on piecework and the more coal I got off the more money I got. So, I was £1 10s better off staying in the mine than going back to Rees' and that was a lot. Occasionally, Rees' would ask me to go up and help and I did that for about two years after the war. I did the odd shift to help out particularly when it came to Christmas. At Christmas time various people would bring their own cakes to the bakehouse to be baked for them and I remember helping out on that. [HM]

Crunch crunch crunch –

blackpats

Sometimes I used to go up [to Rees' Bakery] on a Friday. They would put the dough down and we would finish at five o'clock. Then the dough would rise so I had to go back at half-past seven to punch it and knock all the air out

before it rose again – that was ready then for the night shift coming in. Now, when I used to go to the bottom bakehouse as I walked in you had to go about five yards to the switch and as you were walking it would be crunch crunch crunch and you'd be stepping on blackpats. You'd put the light on and they'd be scurrying everywhere. [HM]

Angel cake and weevils

We used to do a special line. People used to queue up for it. It was called Angel cake. It was a delicacy, people used to go for that. Apart from the ordinary flour, the eggs and the milk powder, you used to have cornflour to bind it together. We kept the cornflour in a big bin but before you used the cornflour, you had to put it through a big sieve. You'd get a few shovelfuls of cornflour in the sieve and you'd shake it and there'd be all these little white weevils in the cornflour and you used to have to throw them out. But people used to enjoy the cake just the same! They wouldn't get away with that these days. [HM]

Off to Bath in service

I decided then that I'd go to service because our Dad was unemployed and we were on the means test and if I had any money coming home that would be taken off his dole. So, I went to work in Bath in the Royal Crescent for a Mr Goold. It's fabulous there. It's like a royal palace inside, full of antiques. The front looks nothing but it goes way back with tremendous huge rooms and his bedroom was almost like a cathedral – that's how I used to think of it. We were on the very top floor of all and not only that. All the other rooms had radiators but we didn't, we had nothing. If you had a glass of water at night and you put it on the chest of drawers to the side of the bed in the morning in the winter you'd have all ice on top of it! [RM]

Nothing to be toffee-nosed about

I was a house parlour maid when I started and I was there for a couple of years and the war broke out. When I started I had ten shillings a week with one half-day and a Sunday off once a month. When my boss's daughter and all the governess, the nursery maid and the children came to live with us because of the war there was all this extra work and I thought to myself, 'I

don't know, this is an awful lot of work for not getting any more money'. So, I mentioned it to the cook and the parlour maid said it's not good bothering, you won't get it and I was quite cross about it. The crunch came one day when the governess said she'd like her meals brought up (that would be on the fourth floor!) I had enough work on, so I said, 'I'm not going to do it, I'm sorry but you'll have to come down and have your meals with us'. She was so annoyed that she went to my boss and told him and I was called into the library and I thought, 'Oh, I'm for the high jump here'. I explained and said I was doing all this extra work and I didn't think it was fair. I'd got plenty of ordinary work on without waiting on her and he said, 'What if I give you a rise in wages?'. I said, 'No, thankyou, sir! I'd prefer not, for the simple reason I don't see why I should keep going up and down the stairs for her'. We all had a rise after that and I still didn't go up to her. So, I quite won that battle. I was very pleased because she was toffee-nosed and she had nothing to be toffee-nosed about. [RM]

'Have you any followers?'

My cousin worked in this house first. That's how I got the job and I said, 'I can't do it'. I had no idea where all the knives and forks went. I was terrified, because we only had one knife and fork at home. She said, 'You'll have the interview and I'll tell you what to do and what to say'. But one thing she forgot to say was this: he was interviewing me now and he said, 'Have you had experience?' and I said, 'Yes'. 'And one thing,' he leaned towards me, 'Have you any followers?' I thought, 'What does he mean?' I said, 'I beg your pardon, sir'. 'Have you a young man?' Thank God, I knew what he meant then. I said, 'No, sir.' 'Well, I don't want you bringing anyone around here. Now, that's got to be understood.' I never had a clue about that but anyway I got the job. My cousin was getting married so she wrote out three great big long sheets of foolscap with all my duties on and that was a great help to me because I wasn't experienced in a big house like that. I was right in at the deep end.

You had a morning uniform, blue and white and you had an afternoon uniform – the nippy hats, a navy dress and a little tiny pinny in the front with a bow tied at the back and little things I wouldn't mind having to this day such as celluloid cuffs which were great when you were washing up. You could slip them on and you'd keep your sleeves lovely and dry. That was great that was.

I got on very well and I never regretted it. The only thing I wish I'd done was learn to be a cook. When my boss died, I came home. I had the shock of my life so many months after when a letter came for me with a year's wages in. He'd left me and all the staff a year's wages. I had about £40. I remember I bought our dad a suit from the 50-shilling tailor on the corner by the Foundry Bridge. [RM]

Off to Malvern in service

As we got to the age of fourteen off we had to go into the world to make one less mouth to feed and, no matter how small our wages, we were expected to send money home every month. My first job was at No 7 College in Great Malvern as dormitory maid. The children at the college were the children of wealthy people and I'm sure they hated being there as much as I did. Up at 6.30 every morning and two hours spent in the sewing room every afternoon. I worked like a slave, darning dozens of woollen socks which seemed to be more darn than sock. Those holes were as big as a cup but I was told socks were only replaced once a term, so I cobbled them up as best I could. I can honestly say the only good thing about that job was the food. For the first time in my life I had enough to eat. After two years there I took a job at Maesllwch Castle, Glasbury-on-Wye. This time I was under-housemaid with two housemaids over me. Work started at 6.30 in the morning – off to collect your grate box. This was the box which held enough wood to lay three fires. This was prepared the night before when I had to go to a very large outbuilding with loads of branches of trees off the estate. On the flap of the wood compartment was a tray which held all the brushes, dusters and a grate sheet which had to be laid over the carpets before work started. To get to any of the rooms was a bit of a nightmare. It was always pitch dark and I had to feel my way to the nearest gas jet. The lady of the house was Mrs de Winton. [EW]

Jim Bolt the blacksmith

We walked to school and that was full of interest because we passed shops on the way, the bakery and the brewery. Most interesting of all to us

Aberbeeg, 1930s. In the centre is Courtney Edmunds' shop and right is Manchester House.

was the blacksmith. There was a blacksmith's shop right on the square in Aberbeeg, in what had been stables for the brewery. The blacksmith was a man by the name of James Bolt. He was a very strong man, short, thick-set, with a big leather apron and shirtsleeves rolled up above the elbow. He was a bit irascible by temper – you didn't know how you'd find him. Sometimes, he was friendly to a degree and sometimes he'd send us packing. We used to love to look through the open door especially when we were coming home in the afternoon and we had a bit of time. We'd stay there watching him hammering away shoeing horses or putting a ring on a cart wheel. This was quite enthralling for us children and sometimes if he wanted to blow the hearth up to get a white heat he'd ask one of us to pull on this big bellows. We were delighted to do that. [RR]

Faggots and peas

When I was about seven or eight in the dinner hour on a Friday I used to go up to the shop in the next street [now New Woodland Terrace] to Mrs Wilde (one of her sons is about now, Trevor Wilde). She used to make faggots and peas on a Friday and sell them. We'd go up with a big jug and we'd have two or three faggots and the peas and they were delicious. They don't make them like that any more. We used to look forward to that. [RR]

Shops in Aberbeeg (1930s)

Of course, we were well off for shops in Aberbeeg then. We had three bakeries – Thomas', James and Day and Kibby's – and they all had grocery shops attached to them. There were several

61

other shops: sweet shops, grocery shops and greengrocers, Poole the newsagents, a post office, butchers. We had Jones the barber. You didn't go in there if you were in a hurry. You had to wait because he used to stop and talk. He liked an audience and was a very loquacious character when he got going. [RR]

Penny bags of sweets from Day's

It was a popular pastime for us children going to school to press our noses up against the glass windows and see what we'd like to have. We only had a ha'penny or a penny if we were lucky. On a Friday afternoon in Day's they used to make up a ha'penny bag or a penny bag. It used to be a mixture of things with different sweets and that was really good value. [RR]

Edmunds' grocer's shop

The grocery shop on the Square belonged to the Edmunds family and the grocer's name was Courtney Edmunds. He had a very good shop there and was a very good businessman. He was always very smartly dressed in a white apron and a bow tie and he often wore a cap. He was very short and he used to stand on a little platform. I often used to like going in there because he was quite a character was old Courtney. There was a fire place in there and I remember seeing an old lady sitting in the corner with a cap on smoking a clay pipe. I think her name was Mrs Arnott. [RR]

I thought I was a millionaire

My aunt, Miss Sarah Parry used to look after the shop in Aberbeeg and sometimes if she went on holiday when I was in my teens my uncle used to ask me if I'd serve in the shop for a week. He paid me £2 for a six-day week [late 1940s]. I thought I was a millionaire. [RR]

The milkman

Of course, it was still the day of the horse and cart. We didn't have a milkman delivering bottles. He would come with his horse and cart and the churns and a hand pail. You'd go to the door with your jug and he'd measure out a pint or a half pint or a quart of milk and you'd have it there fresh every day. [RR]

Christmas baking

Christmas was an interesting time because they'd be busy in the bakehouses baking Christmas cakes. I used to love to call in at my gran and uncle's business coming home from school watching them icing the cakes. Later on, nearer Christmas, the bakers would have a day when the public could bring in their cakes in for baking. They were always very nicely done in the big steam ovens there and I remember my mother always used to make big tinloaf-sized cakes and we'd take these down after lunch and the bakers then would put them in the oven and keep an eye on them. You used to pay sixpence or something for the baking so the bakers would eventually have a pound or two for their pains. Later, on Christmas Day, they did the same thing with poultry. It was a common sight to see people walking down with a big cooking tin with a chicken or turkey covered over with a nice white tea towel. Nine, half-past nine, on Christmas morning people would start going down. They would pay the baker about a shilling or sixpence a bird. They seemed to do better in the bread oven than in the stove at home and, of course, you didn't have to worry about it. There was always a lovely smell when they were baking bread or cakes and on Christmas morning you could smell the poultry cooking when you came up the road from the square to Woodland Terrace. [RR]

British Nylon Factory

A few of the girls did go to the nylon factory in Pontypool and such places simply to get a bit more money. But I was always a practical girl. I thought living locally I could come home to lunch. By the time you bought your lunch and paid your fare to Pontypool you wouldn't be much better off.

Selling salt

We sold our own salt, we used to have great big blocks of salt and when my Dad thought I could be trusted, he gave me the big saw like you'd saw wood with and, it was lovely, we'd saw it all up into about four-inch blocks. There was no such thing as packet salt in those days. The salt used to come in a three foot long by a foot wide block

and we used to cut them into four-inch blocks and then down through the centre so that you had an oblong of about seven or eight inches by five inches, all for tuppence. [EW]

The landowners

I enjoyed working in the solicitor's office because you'd get a packet of deeds and you could literally build up a family tree. Some houses had never left a family and had gone from father to son and so on. To my mind conveyancing isn't as interesting as it used to be.

Many years ago there were interesting things. I mean in certain parts of Abertillery you had to undertake that you would never sell wines and spirits because the land originally was owned by Webbs Brewery and they hadn't wanted anyone in competition selling wines and spirits. One side of the river was Brewery land down as far as the bottom of Alexandra Road and up as far as Somerset Street. Then, from Somerset Street up to Cwmtillery, part of it was owned by Powell's Tillery Steam Coal Company so there all the mineral rights were reserved. If you found a seam of coal in your back garden, that belonged to Powell's Tillery. Up in Cwmtillery was the South Wales Colliery and there you couldn't be a tallow maker [candles]. All this was set out in your deeds that you couldn't do these sort of things. Beyond the river down Six Bells and Arael Street that all belonged to the Pontypool Park estate.

Houses were generally sold leasehold which usually meant you leased the land for 99 years. In Abertillery many of these leaseholds started between 1900

Last day of the hay harvest, Gwaelod-y-gelli Farm, West Side, Blaina, c. 1920. Right of picture are Mrs Vi Harris (on the ladder) and Mr George Harris, headmaster of the 'Cock and Chick' School (holding the rake). To the far left stands a William Carnock, who, it is thought, was a former German POW who did not return home after the end of the First World War.

and 1910. Freeholds are now being purchased but the restrictions on selling beer and so on will still be in your freehold deeds if the land at one time belonged to the brewery. [JL]

The Wallace family

My father was born at Blaentillery Farm in 1885 and my mother was from Woodland Terrace, Cwmtillery. They married in 1910 and then came to Ty Arthur to live. Mum went home then to have her first baby, my brother, and he was born in 1911 and after that she never moved from there. My grandfather, Morgan Wallace kept Blaentillery Farm. His father, Joseph Henry Wallace, was the first-ever Chairman of Abertillery Council. My grandfather was never interested in the farm. He was what they called a gentleman, he was in the lucky position, he didn't have to work for a living. It was my father who wanted the farming and he didn't want anything else at all, so his grandfather gave him £200, a lot of money then, and he said, 'Now get it out of your system.' So, he went to America and he was going to make a fortune. I think the crossing was about a month and he was out in America and back in two months! He started off with this £200 and he went from strength to strength because it was the only thing he ever wanted. He never had a holiday in his life but he was the only man I've ever known who would say his life was one long holiday. He was doing exactly what he wanted to do and it isn't many people who can say that. 'If I could have my time over again I wouldn't make any changes', he said.

We kept Blaentillery until Robert McAlpine bought it from Dad for a tenant farmer. And the man he bought it for (Mr Arthur Jones), well, his son is still there now. Crawshay Bailey was once the owner of Blaentillery Farm and it was a hunting lodge with kennels there and the picture of Crawshay Bailey which hung in the museum came from there. My dad always said it will never come from there as long as I own Blaentillery.' [MD]

Riding sidesaddle to Blaenau Gwent chapel

We used to go down to Blaenau Gwent in the summer and then up here to our chapel in the winter – Bournville, where the DIY place is. My grandmother Wallace, who farmed at Blaentillery, was the oldest member in

years and, I think, in service at Blaenau Gwent and there was a post which was kept for her outside because she used to tie her horse up there. She was only a little tot and she always came down from Blaentillery sidesaddle. When she was quite young she was thrown from a horse and she used to more or less walk on her ankle. In those days they didn't do much about it. She was badly crippled and she would go to Brynmawr every so often to have a pair of boots made. From the ankle down, because it had been dislocated, they were what they used to call melton [strong cloth normally used for overcoats]. [MD]

My father never shaved himself in his life

He [Joseph Wallace] used to go three times a week down to the bottom

Harvesting in Blaenau Gwent.

of Oak Street. There was a barber there (Harold Brown) and he used to go by horse and tie up outside to go and have his shave. When Dad retired, my brother lived in Bournville and he used to come over every other day to shave him. Never shaved himself, daft wasn't it? My father used to scramble to finish his milk round, have his shave and then up to have a game of billiards or snooker at James' billiard hall in Blaenau Gwent. He lived to be 86 and never went to hospital. Towards the end he was failing and they took him in for a few tests and the only thing wrong was a hiatus hernia he never knew he had. [MD]

2,000 head of sheep

We had sheep mainly... we kept a couple of horses for our riding but sheep was our mainstay. We had the largest single flock in South Wales and when we had our sale it was about 2,000 sheep. They were running between Blaentillery and Ty Arthur when both of the farms had the mountain rights and we were entitled to turn the sheep out on the mountain. Someone asked my father one day, 'What would you do, if you won a lot of money?' 'Buy more sheep,' was the answer. In the late '50s Franklyn Engleman from *Down Your Way* came here to this house to interview him. [MD]

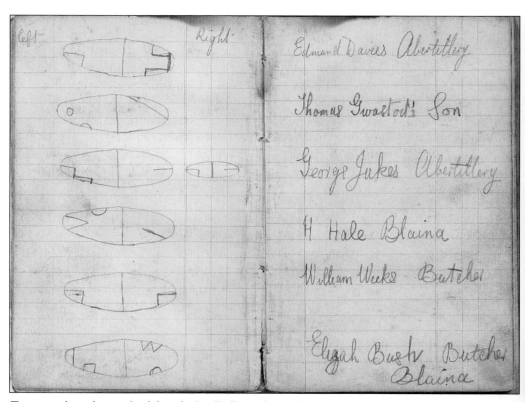

Two pages from the notebook kept by Joe Wallace of Ty Arthur Farm, the local hayward. This book carefully recorded the different ear marks used by owners of sheep to identify their animals.

The end result of what may have been a local shearing contest, c. 1900.

The hayward

My father was in charge of the ear marks for the sheep. The sheep of every farm were given an ear mark and every sheep bought in was given the mark of the farm. Certain farms had the rights to the mountain and if sheep were found up there without permission Joe Wallace would sort them out. He was the hayward. No two ear marks were the same. Every now and again a policeman would come up to the farm with a sheep which had been killed on the road. 'Mr Wallace, will you tell us who this sheep belonged to?' They'd have the two ears in their hands. 'Now, which is the right and which is the left, boy?' At first they didn't know and then it was very difficult to sort them out so dad taught all the policeman that were coming, 'Now if you cut the right one off, put it in your right pocket and the left one in the left pocket. Then, I'll guarantee I'll tell you everyone you bring.' [MD]

The last night of shearing

Tom Sharren lived up in Blaina, he was a councillor at one time. Now he couldn't really play the piano but he could vamp a few notes and it was all covered. We usually had four days shearing and on the last night they used to have this singsong and my mother used to make a lot of wine – she was an excellent wine maker. My grandmother owned the Globe pub in Blaina but never kept it, it was rented out. Well, they used to have lovely glass barrels for brandy and whisky so when they took the licence off the pub we had those. We used to fill these things with wine for the men and if they didn't want cider we used to make them sing. They were happy times. [MD]

The organisers of sheep dog trials at Ty Arthur Farm, c. 1926. Among those pictured are J.H. Wallace, T. Sharren, F. Thomas and T. Jukes.

Dipping

The men would come from the other farms and they would usually bring one or two children with them if they were available. Those sons used to be my age, of course, so I used to be looking forward to these boys coming. Mr Morris from Pencrug Farm over Cwm way had 19 children! If only we'd had a camcorder when the men used to gather in all the sheep. The men had their points where they had to be at a certain time and if only one of them was late the sheep had gone through and my father would blow his top. They used to bring them down to a certain spot and then they'd have to be washed. We had a our own dipping tub up at the Coed-cae [pronounced locally 'Cotcha'] Farm. The farmers got together and put some money in and they had their own dipper

built and a policeman had to be on duty for however many hours you were working to make sure that every sheep went in and each sheep had to be in the tub for about a minute. Now, it's not even compulsory and they wonder why there is so much scab about. [MD]

Once a year at Aberbeeg they used to have the sheep dip just where the filling-station is now on the left-hand side. They used to hold sheep sales there, too. In the summer, they used to dip the sheep in a big square pool by the side of reservoir. We always used to go up after school to watch this because it was the highlight of our year. One year this boy, Tommy Arnott, fell in and they kept dunking him all the time thinking he was a sheep. Poor old Tommy. It was a long time before they realised he wasn't a sheep. We had such a laugh. He came up smelling very sweet. [EW]

Sheep dog trials

They used to come from all over South Wales to that. It was in our Big Meadow Field at Ty Arthur, on the left-hand side going down. It cost sixpence to go in and there were hundreds there. It was a big day in the calendar and entries were to be sent to Edmund John Andrews (Gladys Andrews' husband), Mount Pleasant Farm. My father would never let them pay any rent for this day. It was always his pleasure to give the field and when they finished up they gave my mam a rosebowl and a lovely tea set. [MD]

A pint of milk for the colliery cats

It was only in my teenage times that we had water brought in the house or the electric light, Before we had Aladdin lamps, paraffin. There was a water spout in the yard. We had a bath there where the water used to come off the mountain. When Jack did the milking, the milk never came into the house it was always straight in churns and into that water to cool straight away. The ostler at Rose Heyworth used to come up here every day for a pint of milk for the cats and we used to send the bill in once a month. Milk then was about tuppence ha'penny a pint. The toilet was across the yard and if it was raining you got wet going there. [MD]

The bull in the field

We used to come up on the last train (10.50 p.m.) Abertillery to Bournville halt and I had to walk back down to the farm. If the weather was very bad for walking down there the boys that were getting off at Bournville they very often walked me down as far as the farm because we had no lights at all. I had a little pencil torch and I used to keep that down by my side and I used to go along with my one foot in the gutter – that was my guideline. One time, it was a nice night and the guard said, 'I'll tell you what. We'll stop now by the farm, but don't tell anyone about what I'm doing for you' and I jumped down and waited for the train to go out of sight. But I couldn't go the short cut because the bull was in the field! We were allowed to put the bull in that field, we couldn't put it the top side of the road because there was a footpath through it man-made by the miners themselves. It wasn't a public right of way but my father would always allow them to use it. They could go then through our yard to the Rose Heyworth pit. [MD]

The end of Ty Arthur Farm

Ty Arthur was a council farm, Blaentillery was ours. My dad was a tenant farmer. Luckily, he was at the age (about seventy). He wouldn't have retired, mind, but he was very easy-going, he accepted it and that was that. We just kept one cow, enough for the house. We always used to say that that was 'our rice pudding cow'. The colliery kept the farmhouse for about two years and it was an office for the people who were running it and then it was pulled down. But I could walk down this old road and I could put every brick in place and as long as they leave the fields on the left-hand side and the trees where they are I'm home. There was a white gate and from there on we used to call it our lane and there was a beautiful May tree and it was pink. Then our stile was opposite that. The retaining wall was my pride, all that facing the farm was full of trailing plants that I done. All beautiful colours, I was always a fanatic with my flowers.

One of the old school

My gran died in 1939, just as the war started. She was one hundred. She spoke Welsh fluent but she couldn't read or write; she didn't have any education and she learnt the Welsh language off her parents. This will tell you how old she was: she used to tell me that when she worked as a serving girl on the farms when she was young she used to carry the milk from the Arael Farm and from Pen-rhiw-lech Farm to Aberbeeg down to the railway. She had one can in each hand and one on her head and she used to carry the water back from the spring the same way. When she put the can from her head down there'd be as much water in it as when she'd filled it. She wouldn't waste a drop. When she was in her nineties [1930s] she still used to carry her groceries up from Six Bells like that on her head, up to the Travellers where she was living.

She used to smoke a clay pipe and she'd have a glass of beer if she wanted.

She was taken ill and father decided to get Dr Conlon up from Six Bells. He came and said, 'Oh, the old lady's got a bit of a cold, she'll be alright, though. I'll give her something'. He noticed, then, the old lady getting the pipe out and he said to father, 'Whatever you do, don't take that pipe off her, nor that glass of beer. Because if you do that'll be the end of it.' So, she smoked up to a couple of days before she died.

Another thing she used to do was make patchwork Welsh quilts by candlelight with her little glasses on. When she would run out of thread she'd get some more and although she only had one tooth she'd break it off on that. Then, she'd hold out the thread to the needle and the light and she'd thread him first time.

My brother and I were working nights at Blaenserchan Colliery. We came home this morning and there was no shout at all down from her. 'Bore da,' she always shouted down when she heard us. 'Oh, the old girl's asleep, I expect', so we didn't bother her for a minute or two and we got on with making our breakfast, making tea. I said, 'I'd better go up and see how she's looking'. I went up and she was dead in bed. No disease of any kind just the big age. A wonderful woman. [BH]

CHAPTER 4

Experiences of war

The South Wales Borderers

A third Welsh battalion was offered up to perish on that awful day. The 7th SWB nobly stormed up through the haze of battle. Then, all at once, the haze [the gas] lifted and they were left exposed in the open to sweeping, overwhelming fire as they charged. A party of the Welshmen ran up the slope and fell dead amongst the broken rocks. Of the whole battalion only one officer and some 18 men were alive at the end of the day. All night unheard in the tumult of the new bombardment wounded men were crying on the hillsides or down the ravines. Whatever Sir George Mills now thought of his own plans he must have been gratified by the behaviour of his troops. Those troops had been flung against a position which no infantry in the world could ever have taken and they had proved themselves good soldiers. Two entire brigades had been practically annihilated. The General Officer Commanding the

Chief Allied Armies of the Orient mentioned the 7th Battalion, South Wales Borderers, a battalion animated by a remarkable spirit and lofty sense of duty. On 18 September 1918, under the leadership of Lt. Col. Burgess, it attacked the enemy positions climbing a steep slope under a hail of shells and fire of the trench mortars and machine guns. In spite of the heavy losses, it pressed on with no thought but to reach the enemy and thereby to give proof of its tenacity and offensive spirit and formed an example of self-sacrifice worthy of the highest praise. Francois Desprit.

[18 September 1918 recommendation for the Croix de Guerre awarded to the 7th Battalion of the South Wales Borderers which contained the father of George Morgan]

The Croix de Guerre was established on 8 April 1915 by the French government to commemorate mentions in dispatches both to individuals and to units.

Gassed in the First World War

He suffered from the gas attack. He used to shout in the nights, 'Come on, let's get up!' He was living this for a long time, it was close contact, fighting uphill. They were throwing men away. He was gassed and wounded and taken to a Greek hospital. He couldn't work afterwards. One of the walking dead that's what they told me in Bristol. They said, 'Your father's lungs are like two walnuts. It's another one of the walking dead from the 14-18 war. My dad said, 'I'm not brave, you're not brave when you are fighting for your life'. Because of the First World War we lived in poverty. My father couldn't earn his living and we were six children. There was not penny in compensation. When we did apply for him when he was ill they said he'd been out of the Army too long. [GM]

My father always suffered with his chest. In the First World War he was an officer's batman and he had a whiff of gas. It left him with a weak chest all his life but he still lived to be 88. He had to come out of the pit when he was 50 because of his chest and he went to work in the steelworks as a fitter's mate. He was over there for many years. [HM]

My father come from Somerset and in 1914 when war was declared, he walked from Llanhilleth to Somerset to join the Somerset Light Infantry. He could have joined here but his loyalty was still up there. He fought in Flanders, Paschendale, all the big battles of the First World War and he was mentioned twice in despatches. He had it rough though; he was one of only three who come out from his line after Paschendale. He killed a lot during the war and it used to prey upon him. He used to say, 'The only good German is a dead one'. After the First World War they was murderers. They came back home as trained killers and after what they'd seen they didn't care a s**t about nothing. He'd been gassed with that mustard gas and he suffered terrible after the war. He had a job to breathe and dermatitis would come all over him. In them days, they'd use a zinc and castor oil ointment on him, but that was no good, it was only feeding it. Then, they come up with another thing and they put methylated spirits on him. You can imagine that if your back is raw! I seen him running around the house and trying to get up the chimney, he was so bad. He used to have it all over him... it was a terrible complaint. [BSH]

End of the First World War

I was in the Blaentillery infants school. They had the infants school separate and then up a lot of steps was the junior [it has since been burnt down]. When the war ended, we had a tea and a parade around Cwmtillery. Children were presented with a mug each. We sang *Rule Britannia* and had a good time. A number of children were in tears after smashing their mugs. By the time we were going home, it was raining pouring and I run all the way home. An old man was sat inside his front door and called out, 'Come in out of the rain, my dear' That made me run faster! The day the war ended, the sirens were blown and bells were ringing. The children ran indoors for a penny or two to go down Johnson's shop at the bottom of Crook Hill to buy a flag. [MH]

September 1939: the outbreak of the Second World War

I was in the kitchen. There was my grandmother, my mother, my father and my sister and we were waiting for the news to come over on the radio. At 11 o'clock it did come over and my grandmother started to cry (she was peeling the potatoes for lunch) and Mam was upset. I don't think I really understood the seriousness of it. Then, we all went down to the Drill Hall to see the boys who were meeting there. The TAs all had to go to war. There was crowds down there all on the walls. My future husband and two uncles were there in the TAs and we watched them all go off, all upset with them going and my husband has told me since that they only went to Crickhowell(!), down to the camp until they were ready to be sent other places. Life didn't change much for a year or so, then rationing came in. Mam went and bought all this black cotton material which you had to put up to the windows. I was working in Holman's and then the cigarettes started to get short and we used to keep them under the counter for our regular customers. I used to want to go away to the factory to work but my father was never willing. He didn't want to part with us; he didn't want us to be different. I can honestly say that we enjoyed it through the war. There was dancing at the Market Hall and the Drill Hall, we had good times really. I met my husband

when I was fifteen in the Market Hall, so the soldiers I never used to bother with at all. But crowds of them used to come up from Crick-howell, coloured soldiers and all. [AH]

I can remember it quite plain on the Sunday morning. My brother was in the Territorials. He got called up and he was taken up to Three Cocks. My father was sat in the chair and I seen him crying, openly, when the war was declared, tears really coming down his face. That affected me then. In Llanelly Hill we didn't feel the effects of the war because there was never any lights up. We were still in paraffin lamps, there was no modern lamps, no sewerage. There was always a black out with us. We used to grow a lot. If we wanted a garden we just dug it and some had a seam of coal in them. [GM]

It was a Sunday morning. I can remember sitting round the wireless listening to Mr Chamberlain. It was a beautiful day. I was a bit frightened and wondered what was going to happen. The week before war broke out my mother and my sister and I had gone to Weston for a little holiday. My father sent for us. He said, 'You'd better come home because things are looking dark,' and we had to go and measure for gas masks. So we came home. I can remember being quite concerned about it all. I was 15 and I thought to myself, 'Will we all die? Will the Germans come? That perhaps it was the end of life as we knew it'. We didn't know what to expect, you see.

ARP (Air-Raid Precautions) training exercise on Alexandra Road during the Second World War.

The German bombers following the sparks

We didn't have any bombs. They tell me one did drop on the Arael Mountain. When Cardiff had the blitz on there, they came up here and you could here the 'whump, whump, whump', the throb of the heavy load and then the searchlight would go on. I lived in Argyle Street and you could see the lights up in the sky. [HM]

We used to hear the enemy aircraft coming over. They made many attempts to locate Ebbw Vale steelworks. They used to say that that's what they were after. We heard the drone of the plane, a different sound to the British one. They used to follow the trains up from Newport because they could find Newport fairly easily but they couldn't locate Ebbw Vale along the narrow valleys. They used to watch when they were shovelling coal into the firebox. There'd be a light then from the firebox. And they dropped a few bombs between Aberbeeg and Ebbw Vale. One Saturday night they dropped some bombs on the mountain up above the Cwm road and I remember walking up after chapel to have a look and being late for lunch. It was a long walk but there wasn't much to see after, only a few holes in the ground. [RR]

Tom [Bearcroft] told me that when coming home by train from his work in the South Celynen colliery, the train and even the engine had to be blacked out. One night they could hear a plane following the train. The train stopped and did not go on until it was clear. The men thought it was following the sparks from the engine hoping to find the steelworks at Ebbw Vale. [DB]

ARP members practice disposing of an incendiary bomb during the Second World War. The two men in the background are operating a stirrup pump.

Preparations for air-raids

I remember us being issued with gas masks and going to school and as soon as we heard an air-raid warning, which happened quite frequently at the start of the war, we all used to have to run home and we used to have to take a child home. If another child lived farther away they would have to come to our house and go under the stairs. For the air-raids my father made a bed for us and it was six blocks of wood, you know, the blocks which the men used to bring home from the pit and he nailed planks to them. Then, my mother made a mattress and that's where we used to go. At the start of the war we had all the windows taped up so that if the bombs come all the glass wouldn't fly everywhere. Talk about naive, as if going under the stairs was going to save us from a bomb and sticking up the windows was going to protect us from all the flying glass. [JL]

Alan [my younger brother] was a big beautiful baby but war was about to be declared so while Mam was in bed after Alan's birth a man came to fit him up with a baby gas mask. This was a sort of covered in carrycot made of rubber which smelt terrible and wasn't to Alan's liking at all. We all prayed that he would never have to use it. [EW]

In the beginning we used to come down stairs and huddle together but we got tired of that. We had to carry our gas masks, you could be prosecuted without that, and there were our ration books for clothes – the clothing coupons. [MD]

Black eyes from the black out

I remember asking my aunt what difference would it mean now that we were at war. I was a little boy and hadn't heard much about war before. But it soon affected us and it wasn't long before there were changes. All the lights were dimmed, the road lights were out... it was quite common to see someone with a black eye from walking into a lamppost in the black out. I remember we had a little electric thing, like a broach, worked from a battery and it gave out a glow so you could wear it in your coat and people wouldn't bump into you! On a dark night with no moon it was jet black and people did walk into things. [RR]

The danger of the black out

We'd been to the pictures up in the Palace, me and my cousin who'd been evacuated. We were walking home in the black out and, of course, it was dark. When we got down by Carlyle Street we sort of sensed that someone, a man was following us. You could see a bit as the moon used to make some light. It was only when you first came out that it was completely black. So we were saying to each other, 'Oh, our Dad'll soon be catching us up'. We were just talking, making out that we had somebody else coming and we were saying this out loud and we'd stop and these footsteps would stop. We thought, 'Oh dear'. We got a few yards from the front door and I ran on a couple of steps to knock on the door and as I did he grabbed her and pulled her down. My brother ran out and chased him but he ran all the way up over where the black bridge was. We never found out who it was. But there was a lot of it went on in the black out. We were about nine or ten year old. [MY]

I remember the black out and being told off once by the warden as there was a crack of light showing, 'Put that bloody light out!' Old Mrs Blackmore always liked to keep her door open and he used to cuss here saying, 'Shut that bloody door!' [DB]

Now, Daddy, you look like a man!

We got married in 1938, then the war came and my husband was called up in 1941. He come home on leave from Brecon the first time and he changed into his civvies and my daughter, Christine, was only two year old and she said to him, 'Now, Daddy, you look like a man'. She didn't think much of him in his uniform! [MH]

Wartime service: women on the railway

Now, Mr Walter Davies he was the station-master at Abertillery and he was looking for two girls to train and if we could pass and go as a clerk on the railway we would be exempt from national service. Now I would liked to have joined and gone into the VADs [Voluntary Aid Detachment] as I could have got in on my medicine qualification. But I did it for my mother who was ill. I was in the booking office and they trained me and they would send me one day a week to the goods office and from there I would train in the parcels department. Whoever was off ill, I could fill in then. They made me a relief clerk

76

and so I worked every station from Brynmawr to Chepstow. I never knew where I was going from one week to the other. [MD]

Rationing

We had some extra allowance because of the men coming to help us on the farm but because my father was the boss he didn't get it. We had a full-time workman – a Mr Jenkins from Blaina – he was with us for many many years until he died. And we'd have 2 oz of butter and 2 oz of sugar and an ounce of tea extra for Mr Jenkins because he was having food with us. We killed our own pigs so we were alright for bacon, and we cured all our own hams. [MD]

Dog in a shawl

One day when queuing for milk at the Maypole there was a woman in front of me with a baby in a shawl (Welsh fashion). We had been queuing for a good while but just as she came to be served, a little dog jumped out of the shawl! She didn't get any milk. Oh, we laughed about that. [DB]

Feeding centres during the war

I can remember feeding centres being opened during the war. There used to be one down on the end of Vivian Street and Castle Street and there used to be one in Market Street and up Rhiw Parc. I think I went there once or twice, you know the meat ration was so short.

We had an evacuee from London a girl called Joan Prentice and she lived with us for about three years during the war and went to school in Queen Street. [JL]

The British Restaurant

This was in Market Street. I used to love to go up there. I was in the booking or goods office at the station and we were three girls and the rest were older, married men. I used to think it was marvellous when twice a week we'd walk from there to the British Restaurant. They used to give us disks. There were different coloured disks: one for your starter one for your main course and one for your sweet. I forget how much it was, about a shilling, or one and thruppence. I used to think that was marvellous not to have to go home for a cooked dinner. While other women would go home to have chips for their dinner, I always went home to a cooked dinner which people would have killed for really. We always had our plentiful supplies. But I used to think it was marvellous to go out to somebody else's house and have egg and chips for my dinner. Other kids would clamour to come home with me. You had very basic but good food at the British Restaurant. You could have cottage pie and veg. It was a good meal and it was cheap. [MD]

I used to go up to the Express café in my tea-time break. Andrew was there and his mother and father. His father, who knew my dad, was on the saws at Cwmtillery pit and lost all his fingers there. Ma used to say, 'How's that boy [future husband] of yours getting on?'

Opening of the British Restaurant, Abertillery. From left to right: Rev. Ivor Evans, Mr Ben Francis JP, Mr Gordon Jones (Surveyor), Mrs J. Stobo Prichard, Sir Thomas Jones, Cllr Godfery Jones JP (Chairman of the Council), D.R. Davies (Clerk), Cllr Joseph Day (Chairman, Provision of Meals), Cllr Thomas Gale (Finance Chairman), George Dagger JP, MP.

'Oh, he's not too bad.' Then, when I paid for my cup of tea and sandwich she was giving me a packet of ten cigarettes. 'Send him those when you write to him!' [MD]

Actually, we were very lucky around here in the war years. I can't remember going short of anything. I can remember in Thomas', Aberbeeg, where our ration books were, we could have sausage one week and pork pies the next. I can't remember going short of clothes because Mam was very clever with the needle. She'd unpick a dress of her own and alter it.

Dig for Victory

Then food began to get tight, rationing came in, cars disappeared unless you needed one to carry on your business or like the doctor you had an allowance. Otherwise, there was no motoring for pleasure. They were very different times, sweets got short and were rationed. Things just disappeared, no bananas, no oranges, you didn't see them for years, no rice as well. Within a year or so there was really a different kind of food. Big efforts were made to encourage people to grow for victory, to grow their own and use the garden. Lots of ground that had been neglected and left uncultivated was dug up. Potatoes were grown and lots of people kept a few chickens. You had to register to keep chickens, though, so you could get a bit of corn. I think on the whole we were healthier because we ate a lot of freshly grown stuff. I remember my father and uncle had a row of potatoes in the farm on the top of the mountain up at Penyfan. Dic Lewis, the farmer there, planted a long row for us, well over a hundred yards in a big field. We paid for the potatoes and then in the autumn we had to go up and collect them. It was quite a task but we had sackfuls of these potatoes. It was all hands on deck with my brother and I and my father all up there filling these sacks. [RR]

Working for the American Army

We all had to do some kind of war work. I thought I'd like to go into the WRNS [Women's Royal Naval Service] and my family knew the manageress, but she was called the manager, of the labour exchange. She sent for me one day and said, 'Now, they've asked us to supply the American Army'. You had to have tests and everything and go away to Salisbury – that was the conscription part of it. So, I went to Salisbury at the beginning of 1943 and I worked for the American Army and from there we went to Cheltenham. I was working as a secretary to a colonel and then I think it was towards the end of 1944 that we went to London and I stayed there to the end of the war.

The Americans were willing to give us their rate of pay but Southern Command in the British Army, who employed girls and women in the same capacity as secretaries and drivers and chauffeurs to the generals and colonels, wasn't willing to pay the American rates. The Americans weren't allowed to treat British civilians any different than if they worked for the British Army. So, we could have done better but didn't. But we did have some advantages in that we ate in the officers' mess through the day and although we had to pay, the sum was nominal. We ate very good food really.

The waste of life

Ten of us went down from Abertillery to Newport for our medical, of those ten eight were killed in the war. The only two of us who survived was Eric Fowler who went to the war and myself. [HM]

Into the RAF

I was ground crew in the equipment department equipment assistant. I went down to the South Coast after our initial training and I was there until the fall of France in a little station called Warmwell in Dorsetshire training air gunners and so on. Of course, after the fall of France, the South Coast came under bombing attacks and the station had to be moved so I went then in 1941 to Scotland and I spent many months there before I went overseas to South Africa. I spent almost four years there in Cape Town on an airforce station helping the South Africans to build aircraft. I came back in 1945 luckily to St Athan

Jack C. Bevan (second from left, standing on pallet) pictured with fellow POWs in Germany during the Second World War.

and in July of 1945 the wife and I got married. I came out of the force then in April 1946. [WGH]

Jack Bevan POW

Extracts from the diary of Jack Bevan POW 9772 (formerly of No 82 Pantypwdyn Road) written in Stalag 344, 1944-45:

1944
27 Jan: Received first letter of 1944.
29 Jan: Finished early after argument with guard.
11 Feb: First parcel of 1944. Books from *Argus.*
12 Feb: Snowed hard. No work.
13 Feb: Still snowing.
14 Feb: First clothes parcel since Oct 25 1943. No work except snow clearing.
21 Feb: First cigarette parcel from *Argus.* 500 Martins.
4 Mar: Saturday, no work because we done the task in the week.
17 Apr: Went sick on the job with rheumatism.
18 Apr: Went to doctor, got a couple of weeks off.
21 Apr: 2nd big parcel from the *Argus.* 500 Martins.
1 May: Started work after 14 days sick. Very hot.
4 May: Big parcel. 500 Woodbines from home.
18 May: 2nd book parcel from *Argus.*
25 May: Four years now as a prisoner.
15 Jun: My birthday. 25.
18 Jun: Weighed myself. 114 German pounds – 9 stone.

1945
1 Jan: Wrote my last letter home.
22 Jan: No work except for woodcutting. Big scare on with civvies, evacuees and German transport coming through.
23 Jan: No work owing to scare. Heard the guns.
25 Jan: Evacuated from Pechütte at 12 a.m. Arrived in Neustadt at 9 p.m. Lot of snow on the road. Jews dying.
26 Jan: Left Neustadt at 12 a.m. Arrived in Langenbrück 4 p.m. Billeted in church.
28 Feb: Marched from Langenbrück to Freiwalden.
1 Mar: Marched from Freiwalden to Goldenstein.
2 Mar: Marched from Goldenstein to Hannsdorf.

3 Mar: Marched from Hannsdorf to Klein Mohrau.

3 May: Snowing like a winter's day.

7 May: On the move. Left Klein Mohrau, marched to Glasendorf, near Mittelwald. Warm weather.

8 May: Arrived in Czechoslovakia, good reception by Czechs. Okres Rychow. Guards were disarmed and we were set free, Slatina at 1.50 p.m.

14 May: Left Czechs and back into Sudetenland, stayed the night at Saaz.

15 May: Left Saaz and stopped all day on the line. Slow journey.

16 May: Arrived in Karlsbad. Picked up by Yanks, drove to Ellagen. Good scoff.

19 May: Left Pilsen by air for Brussels, left Brussels for Dunsfold. Went from there to Haywards Heath.

20 May: Got new rig out, preparations for going home.

15 Jun: 26. [This is the last entry in the diary]

Capture by the Germans in 1940

Jack Bevan was sent to Belgium with the British Expeditionary Force (BEF) which was cut off by the Germans and forced to surrender in May 1940. He and his comrades had been told that the Germans had broken through, that they were cut off and they were to try to make for Dunkirk. It was every man for himself. They spent some time hiding in a wood which became surrounded by German tanks. Jack had a German officer, who was studying a map in his staff car, in the sights of his rifle, but he was told not to fire as they would all get blown to hell.

After these Germans had moved on, Jack and his mates started out for Dunkirk but as they came out of a ditch to cross a road they were challenged; they had walked into a German machine gun nest which had been well camouflaged. I asked him, 'What did you do?' 'I'm no bloody hero,' he replied. 'I stopped and put my hands up and so did the others.' This was 25 May 1940. [DTB: memories of conversations with his uncle by Don Bearcroft]

Life as a POW

When in a German prison camp Jack was told: 'If you don't work, you don't eat'. When the Germans found out that he came from South Wales and was a miner, he was put to work in the mines. He and other prisoners were in bad shape at this time and the German miners used to laugh at them because they were too weak to lift the ring supports. But, with the arrival of food parcels their health improved. Jack told me that the Germans could smoke in their mines and sometimes gave them fags. Meanwhile, the Russian POWs were in a separate compound and were in a terrible state. They were not in the Red Cross so did not receive food parcels.

At one time Jack worked in a factory and it was during this time that he came closest to being shot. Apparently, he and his mate got friendly with some German girls working there and they were surprised one time by a guard who caught them with the girls in a store room. The guard went mad, cocking his rifle and shouting and yelling at them. They never risked it again; it wasn't worth getting shot for!

At one time Jack and other POWs were working on a farm. They got on well with the farmer and his wife but one day on arriving for work they were greeted with abuse and things being thrown at them so they returned to camp. Eventually, they did go back to the farm where the old couple apologised to them, saying they were sorry but that day they had received news that their only son had died on the Russian front.

Sometimes the SS and the Gestapo did random inspections or searches and the ordinary Wehrmacht soldier was more afraid of them than the British POWs were. Jack was not bitter to the Germans saying there were good and bad the same as us.

Towards the end of the war the allied planes dropped leaflets and on one occasion a fat German woman turned to them and wiped her bare behind with one of the pamphlets. Jack had to laugh at this.

With the advance of the Russians the Germans kept them on the move [see diary] away from the front. The POWs did not want to be released by the Russians as they could be conscripted into their ranks. When Jack and other POWs were set free by Czech partisans, their German guards were given a hell of a hiding. They could not stop them as they were afraid of getting shot. Later, while trying to reach the American lines, they were almost starving when they came across a truck that had overturned. They were disappointed that it did not contain food, only a load of small arms. However, after they armed themselves they had no trouble obtaining food. [DTB]

Life on the Home Front with your boy away

In March 1939 Jack joined the Territorials. When the war came he and his butty Cliff Evans were some of the first to be called up because they were TAs. When I met Cliff's mother, she told me that she could knock their heads together as they need not have gone to war: Jack worked in the mines and Cliff in the tin works – both reserved occupations.

Well, Jack was captured in Belgium. Tom (Bearcroft, my husband) and me were going on holiday but I didn't want to go. We didn't know were he was and we were very worried. Then, a letter arrived from Germany saying he was a prisoner of war. We got Worthy Richardson to translate it. It was in German but Jack had signed it and I recognised his handwriting. This was the first we had heard of him. So, we went to Weston in the end.

Miss Gregory, the retired head teacher of Queen Street School took on the job of arranging food and clothes parcels for the POWs. We helped make up the parcels. I packed them and Gwyneth (my sister) took them to Miss Gregory to wait for collection.

When they heard Jack was coming home the neighbours up Pantypwdyn (Charlie Jones and others) put up trimmings and flags on the lamp-posts and railings. He did not arrive on time so some went in for their dinner and that's when he appeared. He was very thin when he came home. The neighbours and family all clubbed together and put on a spread in the Bush Hotel for him and Dad gave a speech thanking everyone for their help and for having Jack returned. Tom put our son Donald, who had been born in 1943, into Jack's arms saying, 'This is your nephew who you haven't seen'. He then went on one of the army's retraining schemes and trained to be a plasterer. But he was in poor shape after his experience and never really recovered his health or character. He had brought a trumpet home with him which he had bought off a dance band leader using his cigarette rations – Jack didn't smoke. He had had trumpet lessons with this chap in the camp and he used to play it in the house afterwards. [This trumpet is now a treasured possession of Mr Don Bearcroft, Jack's nephew.]

My mother [Emily Bevan] never cried when he went to war or when he was away but when Jack arrived home she cried floods of tears. An old gipsy had told her not to worry as her son would come home. Old Mr Albert Pope said afterwards, 'I don't know if it was your mother's faith or what, but she always said he would come home'. [DB (Doris Bearcroft, Jack Bevan's older sister)]

War work at the munitions factory

In service our wages were very low and my sister Millie and I began to get restless wanting to earn more money. We both decided after checking with Mam and Dad to sign on for war work thinking that the grass is greener on the other side. But we were to be sadly disillusioned. Wages weren't that good at Bridgend Munition and since it was too far for us to travel home to Aberbeeg we had to stay at a hostel which ate up most of our money. One thing we were grateful for is that a great many of our top actors and actresses of the day joined CEMA [Council for the Encouragement of Music and Arts] so every week or so we were able to see stars like Dame Wendy Hiller, Googie Withers, the Ballet Rambert, the Ballet Russe put on these wonderful plays and ballets for us and for just a few shillings. I lived for dancing in those days and was quite good at it. All Saturday evening dances were evening dress dances. How much more attractive it all was and so much more romantic. We were never short of partners either. We had the Army and the Air Force to choose from!

One day I collapsed at a bus stop in Coventry (where I was billeted for war work in Rugby) going to work and the next thing I knew was that I awoke in hospital to learn that I had pneumonia and pleurisy. After spending several weeks there I was sent home. I was out of work for over a year attending a TB clinic every week. I felt fine but I had a shadow on my right lung and it was a slow job. [EW]

VE Day

It came over that they had signed and it was the end of the war and we had the next day off. I can always remember it was a beautiful day, the sun was shining and in the night then we finished work and we went to the dance. When we came out of the dance, the Salvation Army band was marching around the streets and we all got in line, everybody, it was like the school walks and we all went round Abertillery with the band playing until about two or three o'clock in the morning. I can cry when I think of that! It was wonderful and we were all singing our heads off – *Brightly gleams the banner* and all this sort of thing. Oh there must have been crowds and crowds of people following behind the band. [AH]

Street parties

I was home when the war ended. We had a party out here in the street. We all got together, piano in the street, we had a sing-song. I remember the tables and more food than we'd had for a devil of a long time and that was wonderful in itself. [RM]

There was quite a lot of activity: parties, concerts and so on. On VE Day I was back in St Athan and they shut the station for a couple of days and I was able to come home and take part in the local celebrations. I remember that there was a big dance held in the Drill Hall, I think it was held by the local Home Guard at very short notice and the wife and I were able to go there and meet all the old friends that I hadn't seen for years. That was a great evening... bonfires were all around on the mountains. [WGH]

Post-war rationing

When I was pronounced fit I went to work at Thomas's shop in Hafodyrynys. In those days, although the war was over, we still had rationing and firms and shops were forced by law to accept at least one person who was disabled so I was lucky to be earning once again and to really like my work. Butter in those days was delivered in large 28lb boxes and the butter itself was wrapped in a very large sheet of greaseproof paper so I would get quite excited if it fell to me to open a new box of butter because small amounts of butter would cling to the paper and I would fold this up carefully and hide it ready to take home knowing it would help with the rations. [EW]

Married after the war

When I got married we were still on rations and clothing coupons. All the family saved up so many coupons and gave me them for the food. I had a second-hand suit. We got married in Blaenau Gwent with Ivor Evans. He used to come and see us before we got married and lay the law down to us about going to chapel. I had a red suit and a red hat with a blue feather in it and he whispered to me when we were lined up for him to marry, 'You know, Renee, "Marry in red you'll wish you were dead" – that's the old saying.' I was quite shocked. Then he said, 'I'm only teasing, take no notice'. [RM]

CHAPTER 5

Childhood and education

Standard 8 at Abertillery Central Girls' School (the British Girls' School), c. 1924.

Happy Days

During my schooldays my happiest memories are playing football and rugby for the school and my father actively encouraging me. When I was about eleven or twelve I was able to get a weekend job carrying out groceries for Peglars in Abertillery. Half a crown for a weekend – Friday and Saturday. But father allowed me to give that up so I could play football for the school. [WGH]

A little boy stands on the steps outside his home, Abertillery, c. 1920.

The British School rocking horse

I can remember starting school, I was nearly five. It was the British School, the infants. The teachers were very strict. They had long black skirts and blouses up to their necks. They were all right but they stood no nonsense. If something went wrong and there was a misunderstanding they put you on the rocking horse and that was supposed to put everything right. [DH]

I lost my prize watch

I had four years' certificates. I was never absent for four years! If you went five years then you could have a watch and I wanted a watch. But something happened. One day my father wanted some cigarettes. There was a club, where the Potters is now, and I had to get double woodbines for him and of course if your father asked you to get something you dare not say, 'No, I won't' or 'can't' because you'd have a clip round the ear or maybe more. So, I went in this club and I was a little boy. The men were being served with their pints and I remember trying to draw the attention of the barman and hearing the bus go by. So I missed the bus back and then I had to bring these cigarettes back to the levels and go up the incline. Of course, by the time I managed to walk down from Brynithel it was about ten past two. Jack Thomas then was the teacher and he said I couldn't have my mark because the register had closed and that was it. So I lost my mark and I lost my watch. But when my father heard this story he bought me a watch. It was a two and ninepenny one in a box from Tom Evans' shop. There was also five-shilling ones and they had a second hand on them. Of course, that was for men or for bigger boys than me. So I had to be satisfied with the two and ninepenny watch which was alright. I had it for years. [DH]

Newbridge Secondary School

All the children from Aberbeeg down as far as Cwmcarn went to Newbridge. We had a bus to take us down. We went at twenty past eight in the morning. When I started to the 'grammar school' we had to pay £7 first term, £4 for the other term and we used to pay 12/6 for the lend of the text books. And then, I think, we had to buy a season ticket it was £2 something a year. When the 1944 Act came in then

Standard I at Queen Street Infants School, July 1929.

the fees were cancelled and it was free transport as well and also dinners were introduced in school and they were two and a penny a week, five pence a day. Teachers' meals were a shilling a day and the children's meal was sixpence for the first child, fivepence for the next child, fourpence for the next child and any other child who came after was free.

I went to Newbridge School by train. I had to pay for that but I had free tuition. I wasn't top of the list but I was third and I remember the headmaster said, 'And tell your Dad, when you go home, that there are only two above you and they are both headmaster's girls.' Dad simply said, 'Good girl.' There was no more fuss made.

Education was the way up and out

My father was quite forward-thinking for his age. My brother, who was 15 years older than I was, was sent to grammar school and through the university, which although it is commonplace now it wasn't then. I'm talking about 65 years ago. I also had another sister and none of us earned any money until we were twenty-one. My sister went to a training college and was a schoolteacher and my father paid for all this. He had these little businesses but as none of it was free it was very hard for him really. He was a very conscientious family man. What he did then is commonplace now but it wasn't then. He educated us all.

I went to the grammar school, it was called the County School then, of course. I eventually left and went to a private secretarial college – Cleve's College in Cardiff, a day college – to train as a secretary. I had an interview and the principal of the college accepted me. I used to travel back and fore every day. My father had to pay, none of it was free in those days. Then I was between 20 and 21 when I got my first job after I'd passed my examinations

Teachers at Blaenau Gwent, 1907.

and I went to work in London for the American Army in the war and I worked in Grosvenor Square.

The examination class

I had to sit an exam and if you passed you went to the grammar school. I came 26th out of about 60 and I went in the 'A' stream, the intelligent half [laugh]. Mr Lewis was the teacher that took us in the examination class and I went up there to Abertillery Grammar School about 1945. I remember having to take a form to school because they started family allowances [c. 1946]. I had a sister younger than me and we used to have about five shillings that was the first family allowance. When I was in Queen Street I used to take sixpence a week and we used to buy a savings stamp and when we had fifteen shillings we used to convert it into a savings certificate. [JL]

Respect for authority

I wasn't brought up to flout authority, I was brought up to respect it. Because my father was an ex soldier, an ex-NCO, and he treated us like his own little army. [GM]

We respected them, believe me, even out of school. You'd 'sir' 'em out of school and I mean 'sir'. [JB]

Discipline at school

If I did something wrong I had the cane in school and if my parents got to know about it I had one off them as well and I'm sure that discipline instilled something into me. I loved my parents because of the respect. I was in the scholarship class down in the British

Children and staff at Gelli-Crug School, 27 June 1928. T.W. Evans the headmaster stands on the left with Mr Jones behind him and Mr Fox to the right of picture.

and it was in the summer and we were having our sports day. I was passing a window and I said to this boy, 'I hope they don't put me in the blinking 200 yards.' The teacher heard me and said, 'Mason, come out here!' and I can feel the humiliation now, how I was made to look a fool. He said to me, 'I thought you didn't swear in the Salvation Army'. I said, 'I haven't swore, sir'. He said, 'Boys, didn't we hear him swear as he went by?' 'Yes, sir.' 'Right, for having your cheek put your hand out!' And he took out his cane and nipped me right on the end of this finger then across my palm and my wrist and I was crying from the pain and being unjustly accused of something I hadn't done and that lived with me for the rest of life. Now that was something that was brutal but on the whole you went into a class and that teacher would have your respect. You dare not mess about in the class, so you were taught better. [HM]

Late for school

I remember going up every morning and afternoon to the school and sauntering up the hill over the viaduct to Aberbeeg school. At nine o'clock, Bill Lewis the head would lean over the railings and blow this whistle. So then we'd go tearing up the hill because if we were many minutes late we had the cane and no question about it. On one occasion, however, we were coming back from dinner and they were tarring the road along by Thomas' grocer shop. The men were wearing big aprons with sacking all wrapped around their legs. They were spraying tar out of a barrel onto the surface of the road and throwing shovelfuls of gravel over it. Then, a steam-roller was going over it and compacting it. It was very exciting for us seeing all this going on, especially the steam-roller. We were so absorbed that we didn't hear the whistle blow and we had the cane. [RR]

A hard school but disciplined

I went to Ty Graig and then to Cwm Dyffryn. We'd come back from the hop fields and me and Maxie Whitlock were good fighters and the best fighters had to fight when you went up there. We had to fight the Corbetts and there are hundreds of them up in Cwm. I'd fight one and then after he'd say 'My brother's going to have a go at you now. So, you'd fight him and then the next brother would have a go. It was a rough school, a hard school. The teachers were very strict and there was one up there, the headmaster J.J. Jones and he could swing a cane better than any person I ever known. My hands have been hot and there was another one there, Paddy Sheen, and his famous phrase was: 'Shilling, I'm going to knock your head through that radiator and make chips of it'. It was a hard school but disciplined. [BSH]

There was plenty of discipline but you couldn't complain. Same with the school. I had many a cut across the hand from the headmaster for being late, for not paying attention but I don't think it ever did me any harm. It taught me to behave better. [WGH]

You were strict with the children, you had to be, but 90 per cent of them would listen to you and, of course, you had the support of the parents. If you told a child off and the child went home and said, the parents would support you because you had probably been to school with them or the grandparents and they would say to the child, 'Oh you must have deserved it'. You did have that support.

Working at Soffryd School

Well in the beginning they were very full because they hadn't built a school big enough and, of course, the houses went up so quickly there was a sudden inrush of children so they had to put up another two classrooms in the yard to cope with them and one place underneath which shouldn't have been a class at all because it was dark. But it was so full of children. They have an infant school over the road now, so that's relieved the pressure.

The kindly headmaster

I remember William Blunt, an old gentleman from Nantyglo and a first-class headmaster and a gentleman. The thing that sticks in my mind is when mother and father and I were going on holiday to Gloucester and standing at the bus stop near the war memorial in Somerset Street when Mr Blunt came past on his way to school. He stopped to ask why I wasn't going and it was explained. 'Well, if you're going on holiday here's something to help you along' – a thruppenny bit. That was the kindly gentleman he was. In 1928 Bryngwyn was changed to a mixed school. [WGH]

School meals

My midday meal I had in school, pea soup very often but they were always hot meals and always thoroughly enjoyed and a big help in those days in the late twenties, early thirties. [WGH]

Coronation street party, Melbourne Road, 1953.

Improvements in education

I remember in 1928 we had a new headmaster Edgar Lloyd and he was commercially minded so that in 1929 he started what he called a commercial class. I was lucky enough to be chosen to take part which is where I started my career, if you like, in accountancy. We were able to take examinations for the Royal Society of Arts in bookkeeping, shorthand and so on and this we did. I stayed there until 1932 and there was a job advertised in the local paper for three junior clerks with Abertillery Urban District Council, one in the accountants department and two in the local gasworks. So we had to sit written exams and I was fortunate to come top of the list when the results came out and I had a choice of jobs. And on the advice of my father and the headmaster, of course, I took the job in the accountancy department where I stayed for many years and I was lucky that there was what I regard as a wonderful chief accountant, Mr Harold Powell, a doubly qualified accountant; he took an interest in me and persuaded me to take a correspondence course for a certificate that would enable me to go in for the professional examinations of the Institute of Muncipal Treasurers. This went on until 1939 when the war broke out. I was ready to sit the first examination of the society in January 1940 but, of course, on 28 October 1939 I joined the Royal Air Force. [WGH]

Conversation and listening

Although wirelesses were about in the thirties, they weren't all that much use. They were cumbersome affairs, usually with wires, accumulators to be charged, and so on. So, in the evenings there was always conversation

Games in the street and the school yard

'Bat and catty' or 'kick a tin' was what we had or we'd roll a newspaper up in string and kick it up the street. That was considered quite good sport. Or we'd put the tin down, kick it away, go and hide, and then someone would come back and you had to dash out and kick the tin again.

As children we played in the street but it was somewhat different to today. There was very little traffic only the occasional horse and cart. Cars were just coming about in the thirties but head lights were poor so they didn't do a lot of driving in the night, normally. Street lights were very different to what they are now. They were about a 60 or 100 watt lamp up on a pole and you just had a pool of yellow light under the lamppost. Then you went into utter darkness till you reached the next lamppost. Normally, we clustered around a lamppost somewhere and centred our games and chasing each other from somewhere like that. [RR]

During the playtime we had the usual games which were favourites in the yards. Marbles was a popular game and so was playing games involving cards. There were cards put in the packets of most makes of cigarettes and we used to like collecting those to try to get sets of them. They had a series of cards on things like railway engines, wild animals, flags, cricketers, cars, all sorts. There was hopscotch which was very popular with the girls, then 'strong horses weak donkeys', 'touch', 'stop and

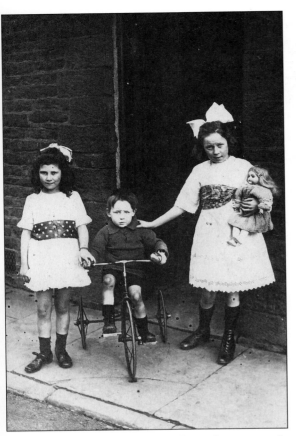

Hilda and Dan Samuels and Miss Berrow outside 'Twg' Samuels' pub – the Castle Inn, Abertillery, 1920s.

and you learned to listen as a child and were involved in quite a lot. There were no record players and television sets. We listened to our aunts and great aunts and uncles telling us of various things and what was going on all around. It was very interesting and I look back with a great deal of pleasure at those days. It was very often a case of being seen and not heard. They'd say: 'Be quiet now', 'You listen!', 'We're not talking to you.' But you learned a lot by listening to older people talking. [RR] release'. The yard was a hive of activity during the playtime. [RR]

We played 'strong horses and weak donkeys', 'scotch and tag. There was skipping and bouncing the ball up against the wall and jumping over it, leapfrog. 'Arch and tunnel' was one game we used to love to play, also 'whip and top', and 'Jack across the water'. You'd have a team here and a team there and somebody in the middle and the one 'Jack across the water' would try and catch them.

I remember when we used to play bolly and guiders and 'whip and top' oh and hopscotch. 'Bat and catty' was magic. You couldn't do it now because of the traffic. The windows we used to break in those days was nobody's business. They'd come to the house and say, 'Your Eileen have broken a window. Seven shillings!' My father used to go berserk and those panes of window always cost seven shillings so I didn't break many I can tell you because we used to get a hammering. [EW]

Exercises and keeping warm at school

When the whistle went we had to get into our classes standing in straight lines in the yard. In the winter then we did exercises to warm ourselves up as it wasn't much warmer in the classrooms than it was outside. We'd be running on the spot, arms raised, legs raised and so on to get the circulation moving. They were typical old class-rooms with double desks arranged in rows and there was the teacher's desk at the front and an open coal fire. If you were in the front row you got some of the heat from the fire but if you were at the back it was the afternoon before you got warm. [RR]

There were no after-school activities at all but at Christmas time we did have a party but we always had to sit at our desks to have this bit of cake. We used to have free milk when we were in school and during the winter they used to put these crates of milk in front of the fire to warm so it was always a bit, ugh, tepid and in the winter the ice used to come and I always remember the tops sort of popping off because of the ice. There was a coal fire – that was all that used to heat the schoolroom – and the teacher used to sit mostly in front of it and we never felt any of the heat! [JL]

'Fatty Arbuckle'

I went to Aberbeeg School. I was plump they tell me when I was young, I can't remember it now. Somebody called me 'Fatty Arbuckle'. To walk up that hill to Aberbeeg School was agony for me. I used to catch hold of the railings pulling myself up and old Mr Martendale used to be up in the school yard and be bellowing down at us if we were a little bit late. And to go to Sunday school after a big dinner up that hill again it was cruel. I was terrified of the teachers except for Mr Ken Lloyd. Mr Lewis took over from Mr Martendale and they were horrible they really terrified us. [EW]

Favouritism

They had their favourites. I remember during sewing class Mr Martendale coming in and watching us trying to sew a hankie. There was one pretty girl from Brynithel and he said to her, 'What's the matter?' and she said, 'My hands are sweating'. Her sewing needle kept slipping out and he went to his house, which was the little school house, and he brought her back some talcum powder to rub on her hands, just for her! [EW]

School trip

With Aberbeeg School we went to Southampton to see the last voyage of the *Mauretania* and that was very interesting because once you got on there, well it wasn't like being on a ship it was like being in a beautiful hotel. [EW]

Camping holidays

We used to go camping before the war. We went by train and the bus used to meet us at Barry station and take us out from there. I went twice to winter and summer camp which was at Rhoose. We went just before war was declared in the July [1939]. Two teachers would come with us and we used to have lovely times. It all came under the county. They paid for us to go. We had big, long dormitories with double-decker beds, like they call bunk beds now, and you had to go up to the kitchen for food. We used to have concerts and entertainment there, it was really lovely. They had a big square there and the airport is all built over where that was now. The boys used to be at Gileston in a separate camp and one day we walked from Rhoose across the beach, when the tide was right out, to Cold Knap and all the boys were there and we had a whale of a time. They'd treat us to pictures

Gelli-Crug School at camp, c. 1938.

Abertillery schoolgirls at camp in Rhoose, 1939.

and we didn't pay for nothing only our pocket money. We used to have a tuck shop and we could keep in touch with the family. I think we used to go for a fortnight if I remember rightly and we'd have lessons as well. They had one dormitory there which was like a school-room and we'd have lessons there at different times of the day. My schooldays were happy times, I enjoyed them. [AH]

We used to go to Pendine camp for a fortnight. We used to sing:

In Pendine camp we're up like a lark
We go to bed before it's dark
We lay our sleepy heads on our little straw
beds
And we're early on parade in the morning

When you're feeling rather funny with a
pain in your tummy
And you're rather off your food and you're
crying for your Mummy
There's a lady neat and dandy with a bottle
always handy
And she's early on parade in the morning

There used to be porpoises down there and we used to see them in the morning and we had a fortnight on little camp beds under tents. It was marvellous for us. There were no such things as holidays then. [EW]

A day out in The Dingle

Our holidays was a day up in The Dingle where the whole family went except father and we'd take up kettles, pots and tarts and everything you could think of. We built our own fire and the children would make their own little dams and pool. It was really a day out and it seemed a long walk. Now I'm older, I know it isn't but it seemed a long walk to me then. But it used to be magic and Dad used to say, 'Now, bring me back a flagon of spring water, bach' because it used to be gorgeous and the spring is still running there at the entrance to The Dingle. There was all this beautiful greenery and although it was forbidden the big boys used to climb

95

Picnicking in Cwmbeeg, 1920s. Among those pictured are Olive Jenkins, Maggie Jones, George Stockholm, Bernie Jenkins, Bertha Jenkins, Liz Parry (little one) and Gladys Turner.

over and swim in the reservoir. [EW]

The magic lantern show

It used to cost a ha'penny to go into this magic lantern. What stands out most in my mind is this: we had two big stoves in the Army and, of course, if the wind was in the wrong direction you'd be there coughing and spluttering because of the smoke. On this one occasion [c. 1932] they put on a shadow-graph. To do that you put a great big sheet up and they shone a light from behind the sheet and people performed behind it so their shadows would be casting onto this sheet. Some of the older bandsman were carrying one of the fellows, laying him on a table, and then there was this man coming down with this knife and sort of cutting him

open and bringing out a string of sausages. I was astounded, I thought, 'Ooh, what have they done?' After it was over I remember going to my uncle and saying to him, 'Who was that?' and this man by the name of Les Hobbs said to me, 'Did you see it, my son?' I said, 'Yes, what happened?' 'Well that was sausages from inside him' and I said, 'Who's the one you put the knife into, then?' and he pointed and I can remember looking over and in my innocence I thought how hasn't he got a bandage on!

Mainly it was biblical stories on the magic lantern and I can remember the story of Joseph and how he was put in a pit and sold to the Egyptians by his brothers and they used to flash up this series of slides. [HM]

CHAPTER 6
Religion

Salvation Army children, 1950s.

The Army was your life

When my grandfather's family had come from the Forest of Dean, they weren't connected with religious life whatsoever but my grandfather got converted and became a Salvationist and my father grew up in the Salvation Army as well. For many years he was the Welcome Sergeant. He wasn't a very learned man but he had a very pleasant nature and he would shake hands with people and make them welcome. I was taken to the Army. They tell me that the first outing from 6 Argyle Street I ever had after being born was in the pram to the Salvation Army. They took me there and I was passed around because I was such a tiny baby. I think I was three pounds something when I was born. The Army was your life and I spent many a happy time there. What we enjoyed as children then, children wouldn't enjoy today but for us it was something special. We would have little games and play around. I started to learn to play an instrument and I was in the junior choir. I was there nearly every day. [HM]

Sunday school trips

Our Sunday school trip was to Abergavenny Park and they'd have races. It was just like a family day out and not even in a bus.

There was a member of the band, name of Cliff Powell, and he had an old lorry in which he had forms [benches] covered over. He used to take people back and fore to Cwmtillery pit in their dirty clothes because in those days they didn't have the baths. We used to clear all this out and that's how we used to get there.

As well as that, I can remember goin to Barry Island in Collier's buses and he used to come over down into Llanhilleth pitch and the bus would stop at the bottom and we'd all have to get out and walk because he couldn't take a bus-load up to the top. When we used to get on Barry Island we'd take the Salvation Army flag and dig it in the sand so if anyone got lost they coul see the flag there. We thought this trip was something great because we didn't have anything much in those days. [HM]

Salvation Army band

It was such a marvellous band in Abertillery and they travelled all ove the country. They were booked up year in advance to go. My whole object, more than anything else, was to get int the senior band but you couldn't get in until you were fifteen, when you transferred from the junior band.

By the end of the war we had youngsters come in and they were fantastic and the standard of playing I would say was certainly the best in Wales, and even perhaps in the West Country. The Army would only allow the band to go away four weekends a year and we went all over the country – London, Manchester, Liverpool, Carlisle, down on the South Coast. The biggest congregation we ever played in front of wa in the Picton Hall in Liverpool and there was 1,200 people there. Not only was the brass band playing but in the band they had a really good male voice

Departure of the Abertillery Salvation Army band from Guernsey, Easter 1914.

party. In the Picton Hall the 18 members sang the Hallelujah chorus and they all stood and for the first time ever as we finished the chorus the audience started to applaud. I can still feel the thrill now, of the shivers going up my back from the emotion and I felt like I wanted to cry because it was such an emotional occasion.

We always went away on a Easter-time and very often in August. I can remember we went to Worthing in 1945 and we had the Lord Mayor come to welcome us. Of course, we hadn't had much in the way of food and they came in with tinned pears and we hadn't seen them for years. This one fella was talk-ing to this one lady and I think he must have created an impression, 'Would you like some cream on your tinned pears?' 'Yes,' and he put the cream on but it wasn't cream it was salad cream! [HM]

I had my knees rubbed out of my elbows

We did have a fellow come from Abercarn to the Salvation Army and in Abertillery you were very strict in your dress, in your deportment, in everything, and when he came he was a little bit below our standard and he had

99

Ebenezer chapel elders, Abertillery, 1920s.

to be told what he was doing. We didn't like the way he conducted himself but as Salvationists you can't really chuck anyone out.

Well, the band always used to have an open-air service on Saturday night outside the Prince of Wales pub, where the job centre used to be. Although it was supposed to be a religious service, the band played and people used to come and listen – nothing much else on a Saturday night. All the way around the path by the church, up to where Ewins the chemist is now, there used to be hundreds of people come to listen.

Anyhow, this fella had come and they asked him to have an evangelical word and, of course, he got carried away. He was there spouting away and everyone was getting so embarrassed at the things he was saying. I remember him saying

his home life was so bad that his parents used to whip him and he exaggerated and said 'I had my knees rubbed out of my elbows' and we thought, 'What on earth is he talking about?' Instead of being in the confines of the ring, he started walking down Church Street so two of the bandsman went up, caused a bit of a scene, but caught him and brought him back. [HM]

Temperance

Dad was strict with us we were never allowed to smoke. My father always told my sister and I if he caught us ever smoking he'd knock the bugger down our throats. But though he was strict it didn't do us any harm. We weren't allowed to go in a pub or anything like

The funeral procession of Mr Gore along Rose Heyworth Road, 1929. He was a leading member of Abertillery Salvation Army.

that, oh gosh no. Even after I was married, if I did go with my husband, if he was having a drink I used to feel terrible. I felt as though I was doing wrong because I'd been taught that way. [AH]

Dead against gossip

Our dad was dead against gossip and Mam was never allowed to stand on the front door. You were never allowed to fold your arms because that looked as though you were going to gossip. He was very very strict, my dad. [EW]

Tabernacle chapel

I was there from the cradle roll. I was in everything – the Band of Hope, Christian endeavour. There was a youth club eventually but I was older then when they started that. There were needlework classes for the older people and Sunday school. Mr Robert Hall

took my mother's class – the older ladies' class – and Mr Isaac used to take the men's class which my father was in. Gertie Hall was in charge of my class. Gradually, you went up from the babies class into the junior then the intermediate. We used to have anniversary and school walks. The school walks was a wonderful day, we used to look forward to those. We had a new bonnet and a summer dress for the Whitsun although we were short of money and Mam was struggling but for the Whitsun walks we had to put last year's on so as not to mess it up. We had to look after it and I'm still the same now, if I come in I got to take it off. We were taught that and you still do it, don't you? [AH]

We always used to go to Tabernacle on a Sunday afternoon and then we'd have a story and they would give us a little pamphlet with a text in and a little prayer to bring home. My sister and I, as children, always had to take this to my grandmother to show her that we'd been to chapel. At Whitsun the chapels were marvellous because practically everybody in chapel used to say a verse and then as my eldest sister could she always used to have to sing. The chapels were absolutely full. We used to have to put chairs down the aisles. I used to go on a Sunday evening when I was a bit older and there was always a choir of men. It was just an ordinary chapel choir but it was very nice. [JL]

Somerset Street chapel

My mother was a great chapel woman in the Somerset Street chapel and her father. There was a chapel up in Newall Street, I was a child when it was closed and my grandfather was the choirmaster and the organist up there (about 1910) and they lived in No 52 Princess Street. We went to chapel went three times on a Sunday and we went to Christian Endeavour. Chapel was a very important thing and my mother's father used to compose his own marches for when they used to march out at Whitsun.

Ebenezer chapel

My great-grandmother Amy Oldland was one of the founder members. She was one of the first converts and was baptised in a pool on the site of the old Vivian brickyard prior to the building of Ebenezer chapel. Ebenezer was founded by a group who, together with the minister Rev. Llewelyn Jones, left King Street chapel. The reason for the breakaway is unknown but is thought to have been over theology. Gran Oldland

collected hymn books for the opening of the chapel in 1877. My great-grandfather William Dykes was a life deacon for many years. [KD]

Chapels in Cwmtillery

There were three chapels on the east side of Cwmtillery. There was Zion and Mr Hammond used to conduct the singing there, Mr Oriel was one of the teachers in the Sunday school among many others. The minister there was the Rev. Thomas Allen. I believe his son became an MP, Sir Thomas Allen. The Celtic Club used to be the Wesleyan chapel. On a Sunday school anniversary people used to stand in the porch, it was crowded. The other chapel, commonly known as 'the Redbrick' started life as the Bible Christians, a sect well known in Cornwall. After a number of years they joined the Methodists and became known as the United Methodists. When I was young we used to call it Bateman's chapel. They were a big family that attended there. What happy memories I have of when I used to be pulled there morning, noon and night even after Sunday school. They had a PSA (pleasant Sunday afternoon) before the evening service. [MH]

The synagogue

Well, Mr Harry Simons, the furniture shop, he knew my grandmother and he told her that she could have one of his houses and that was No 2 Newall Street. But, of course, he was a Jew and they had the synagogue at the back of our house. There wasn't a big

Ebenezer Revival Mission Band, Abertillery, 2 September 1905. From left to right, back row: George Malsom, T. Powell, W. Randel, W. Morgan, W.G. Richards. Fourth row: George Waters (Vice President), W. James, J. Bridgewater, J.T.H. Davies, E. Cuff, W. Stanfield, Dl. Hayward, H. Wheeler. Third row: Mrs Mudway, Mrs Morgan, Mrs Meek, R. Byard, D. Lewis, W. Mudway, Mrs Lewis, J. Williams (Visiting Secretary), J. Davies. Second row: Mrs Powell, Mrs Bridgewater, Mrs Cuff, Tom James, Rev. D. Collier (Pastor), W. Lewis (President), Mrs Davies, Mrs Hayward, Mrs Hawkins, Mrs Pope. Front row: W. Skinner, Miss L. Owen, W. Meek (Secretary), Miss A. Oldland, E. King.

attendance, I think. All I can remember is hearing this foreign language. I had a cousin, who I was brought up with, and we used to try and look through the window to see what they were doing and we got told off a few times. My grandmother always made her own bread, own cakes, pickles, jams, you name it she did it. Now, whenever she made bread, Mr Simons used to knock at the door and say, 'Oh, Mrs Gulliford, why do you make bread when we're coming here? Our mouths are watering!' It was the Jewish sabbath, of course, and they were fasting. The cobs would be on the window and my grandmother would say, 'You can have one if you want to.' 'Temptress!' would come the reply. [RM]

The sanctity of the Sabbath

When I lived with my grandmother I went to the Wesleyans that's

Tabernacle Whitsun walk, 1920s.

burnt down. Then, when I went to live with my aunt I went to Blaenau Gwent Sunday school. I liked living with my grandmother best because she wasn't so strict. With my father's sister, they were very strict and they went to chapel all the week and three times on Sunday. On a Sunday you couldn't do anything, nothing at all other than have your dinner. I always remember once I had a little doll and I was knitting it a little dress. My father's mother was alive then and did I have a telling off because it was on Sunday – I had to sit still and not move, not speak for an hour. That was my punishment because I was knit-

ting on a Sunday. [RM]

I've been a member of Aberbeeg Methodists ever since I grew up there in Sunday school. Mother was never religious but she always made sure that we went to chapel – same with playing on the yard on a Sunday. You could kick a ball every other day bar a Sunday. You had to observe Sunday as Sunday! [BF]

Whitsun walks

This was a big day in the year. We normally had a new suit or clothes for one thing. We had a nice tea in the chapel. With my brother, it was my job on the morning of Whit Monday to carry down a big clothes'-basket with the best china in. My aunts and the other ladies of the chapel would be waiting on the tables and they used to take their tea-sets down and their cutlery and teapots and jugs. Great pride in this, mind. The whole chapel would walk to Llanhilleth and round and back and after tea we would have games in the field in Aberbeeg. Sweets would be given out and tea always seemed to be so nice with the jelly and blancmange and lovely bread and butter and cakes. I can see them making the tea now at Glandwr. Mrs Keeling was doing it at one time and it was made in a big earthenware bowl, reddish-brown on the outside and a creamy yellow colour on the inside. This would hold about five or six gallons and they would have a big muslin bag with half a pound or a pound of tea in and that would be hanging over the side. They would pour boiling water in that. It was a big tea with a few sittings. When I was a boy I expect there were two or three hundred there having tea and so it was quite a venture. Mr Evans, the caretaker, was outside the chapel on a piece of waste ground with a galvanised stove-thing with a fire underneath boiling up the water. The ladies would have plenty of hot water then for washing-up. They had another boiler on the fire inside for making the tea, a big iron one with a handle over the top and a tap on it. It was all go then for an hour and afterwards up to the fields to play games. [RR]

The only time Dad really let us dress up and he'd say, 'You look nice,

bach' was Whitsun because we went to chapel three times that day and that was the only day of the year we ate our fill. There was bread and butter, slabs of plain cake and slabs of fruitcake and you would eat and gorge yourself sick. It was wonderful to be marching all the way down to Llanhilleth and there'd be close on a hundred, I expect, because our chapel used to be full. And we'd be ever so weary, we'd go right down round the horseshoe bend and back and you didn't think you could walk another step. There would be this old lady, Mrs Davies who was too big and too old to walk. She would have stayed behind to help with the refreshments and she'd be looking over the railings in her lovely white apron. 'Oh, there's Mrs Davies, let's have a piece of cake!' And I don't ever remember a wet Whitsun! We wore sandals and they used to stick to the ground and by the time you got back to the chapel you had a half-inch of grit and pebbles on your shoes. We had a new dress, it was marvellous and on Monday morning Mam used to cover our kitchen table with newspaper. Then she would lay out our coats and she'd brush brush brush every speck of dust or hair off, fold them as if they'd come from the shop and put them in the bottom drawer in her room. We were well turned out on Sunday.

After the walks we always went down to the field in Aberbeeg and it was nothing to see a couple of hundred people down there because the Prims used to go down there and we used to go there from Tabernacle. It used to be crowded. Games used to be organised and would go on until it was nearly dark. It was magic, there were prizes for every race. [EW]

Two views of past Whitsuns. Above Cwmtillery United Methodist Church. Below: St Michael's Church, Abertillery.

A tide of young walkers from Ebenezer chapel sweeps over the Foundry Bridge, c. 1950.

We used to come down from Blaenau Gwent chapel all the way down Portland Street to the bridge. It was very popular chapel and in those days, of course, most parents used to send their children or encourage them to go to Sunday school. They used to look forward to the cake and biscuits and whathaveyou afterwards. Oh yes, it was a great day. It's a pity it's diminished now to almost nothing. [WGH]

The annual chapel outing

The other big day in the year was the annual outing usually to Barry Island with the Sunday school, sometimes by train, sometimes by bus. Of course, there were many children then who didn't have a holiday as such, as most people do today. A day at the seaside was as much as a lot of people had. In the thirties there were very few holidays for working people. You knew if you took a week off you had no pay, there weren't paid holidays. People worked a six-day or certainly a five and a half-day week and I remember my father always worked till twelve or one o'clock on a Saturday. [RR]

Japanese style is exhibited by Salvation Army members, 1920s.

The talent in the chapels

They used to have concerts on a wet night or even a fine night in Blaenau Gwent Baptist, of course, it's pulled down now. Two big chapels they were and the talent, oh gosh, it would put the rubbish on the telly to shame. When the strike was on in 1926 they'd have reciting and singing most nights. They went through Sunday school a lot of them. They got their knowledge and tuition but anyway it's a shame that they don't have more of it now. The telly has killed it, of course. In the chapels it was then and you'd go practising for Whitsun and to be in the anniversary. [MH]

Putting on a show

We did several shows up at the Methodists [Blaenau Gwent] same as the amateur dramatics. It was hard work mind because you was very limited and we had to change sometimes over the road. A chap who used to work in Six Bells was the producer – Billy Bryant – and Dai Jones used to help him. *The Wreck of the Argosy* was one, *Pearl, The Fisher Maiden*, another. The one I liked and everybody liked was *Agatha the Gypsy Maid*. We had some good stars and we made our costumes ourselves. I was a sailor in one and I met my wife there because she come up helping with Rachel Price and Enid Williams (Brown now). We courted for nine months and got married and that was it. We got married at Somerset Street in 1936 and I can tell you it was the same price as a dog licence. It was 12s 6d and the minister gave us 5 bob back. My wages then from Cwmtillery were £2 5s. [JB]

CHAPTER 7

Entertainment and sport

The 41 Club on one of its outings.

Percy (left) and Albert Williams of Princess Street, Abertillery, c. 1920.

The 41 Club

Percy and Albert Williams started the 41 Club. They used to meet in the Oddfellows Hall in Queen Street and there was a nice crowd of them and the boys were wonderful. They planned their trips and where they would go – to Rhyl and they went up to Margate, quite a few places. Mam went with them each time. They would save all year round for their holiday, paying so much every month. Then the interest they had off the money would go for all their trips when they were away, they would go for a trip every day. Before they would go, on the Friday night 'Perc' and 'Alb' would take their car and go round and pick up all the cases of the people who were going so they could all be put on Collier's coach to save all the people having to worry about carrying their luggage the next morning. They spoilt their friends who went with them, you know. I don't know why they called it the 41 Club but I think there were 41 people in it. Mr Mason was in it from Salvation Army, Mr and Mrs Jones, Mr and Mrs Baker. [AH]

The travels of 'Perc' and 'Alb'

And during their lifetime they went literally everywhere. They would be sitting listening to the wireless and something would come on about oh something happening in Scotland and they would just pack their bags and they would go. They had a big car and on the back was a big wooden box and they would put their sleeping bags and all their camping stuff and off they would go at just a minute's notice. They were the type of people who would always go up to the big fights up in London. I can remember them going to Freddie Mills. I think Reg Hoskins used to go to the fights. It was probably in the early sixties that the two of them went off to America and in that time it was a really big event for anyone to go to America and I think they were away for about six weeks. [JL]

110

In later years the boys used to alter the cars so that they could make a bed out of the back seat. And when they went off travelling they used to live in the car; they'd have everything fitted in the back of boot – a table would pull out and the back seat of the car would be a double bed for the boys to sleep. They would travel to the back and beyond; they would be right out in the wilderness on tops of mountains and everywhere and they would walk miles and miles and miles. They were very fond of North Wales and Scotland was another place. [AH]

The generosity of Percy and Albert

The day I got married they took me to church in the car and my friend who was bridesmaid wasn't very well and they went down and brought her up to the house because she had TB; they were just there for you. [AH]

A radio set

Many years ago there wasn't many radios around and my father loved his radio. The first radio we had was with an accumulator on a shelf in a cupboard in the kitchen and Dad was very fond of this. Well, the radios were becoming a bit more modern and my father seen one in Stibbs' shop. It was a beautiful set and he come home talking about this radio. My mother wasn't willing, she didn't go it for a lot. She said, 'I could have a bedroom suite for what you're paying for that'. But Dad did

have the radio and it was a beautiful piece of furniture, oh I bet it be the size of this table and all press studs on it. [JL]

Listening to boxing in the middle of the night

They were so keen on their sport – Reg Hoskins, 'Perc' and 'Alb', Cyril Collier – and Dad had this radio and he could get America and all around the world on it so when there was a boxing match in America they would all end up downstairs in our house. Often, it was the middle of the night and they would all congregate in our kitchen listening to this box, anything with sport.

Charabanc outings

Before Barry Island we made an effort to get a farmer to give us a field down in Gilwern so we could have a picnic. That was the first sort of entertainment in the chapel that I remember. We went by bus. First of all it was charabanc and we never used to get there in one go. They used to break down or summat. Then they managed to fix it up and away you'd go again, pushing part of it. [JB]

We went on charabancs. Fred Adams, well he's more well known as a baker on the top of Ashfield Road. But, before then, he used to have a charabanc. In the summertime, it was a big honour to have a ride in this and we used to go down to Gilwern. We even went as far as Crickhowell but he

Blaenau Gwent Workmen's Club trip to Blackpool, 1930.

broke down! That happened very often. The roads then was ruts. All Rose Heyworth Road was big ruts and the charabancs had hard tyres. Coming home you had to walk up the old Rock. Because if the women done a bit of shopping in the big place in Crickhowell we boys had to walk because he wouldn't pull up there with us in it. There was bend there and he wouldn't go round. He'd be chug chug chugging along so we had to get out there and walk or sometimes push behind him. Fred Adams himself ran these trips. I think he used to charge fourpence or fivepence, a boy could go in the charabanc but he had to be accompanied by a parent. It was strict at that time. [DH]

If you had a week off from the pit [Cwmtillery] you didn't get paid for it. So, my father would come over with my mother, my sister and myself for a week and then he would come back home. We used to catch the train from Abertillery to Newport then the train to Stapleton Road in Bristol and then a bus journey out to this village. We would stay there for about three weeks with what we called my 'aunt' and it was very pleasant out in the country. We would go down by the brook and fish and right opposite there was open fields. [HM]

Two pictures from the album of Mr Reg Hoskins capture the fun and popularity of an eagerly awaited break to the South Wales or West Country seaside.

The Fountain Inn in Cwmtillery, c. 1900. It was owned by Chivers Brewery and there was a tunnel underneath the road through which barrels were rolled from the brewery!

Pubs in Cwmtillery

There was the Fountain and then the New Bridgend that's still doing well and the Old Bridgend and the Britannia and then in Alma Street there was the Mount – the Mount Pleasant – that's still there. I don't know why they wanted all them in one area. I know they must have got thirsty with the coke ovens but I mean. In Cwmtillery the off-licence was in Woodland Terrace and then over the other side, it was only the South Wales Inn. [MH]

My father's father, Noah Mason had a wooden leg. They were hard drinkers in those days and I heard my father say that Noah was a real 'outer'.

He lived in a little house, there were just one or two houses up in Scotch-y-du (Coedcae-du). Very often, on a Saturday night, he'd be coming home and if the rain was lashing he'd fall down and they'd go and pick him up the next morning. [HM]

Plethora of pubs and clubs

Oh, the pubs and clubs that were in Abertillery. I used to do some work for the LVA [Licensed Victuallers' Association] to apply for extension for Christmas, Easter and other bank holidays to have an extra half-hour or hour and I think there were 32 in the LVA at that particular time (1950s). [JL]

The Castle Inn, Abertillery, 1920s. The building was demolished in the 1960s.

Eddie Howells and Ken Brickell (in his trademark trilby) share a drink and a laugh in the 'old' Mitre public house, 1960s.

The day they allow a woman into that club

Every night without fail, at about eight o'clock he would go out to the wash-house, have a wash under the cold water tap, then brush his hair in a small mirror by the back door, always humming tunes such as those sung in the men's choirs. Then came the white silk scarf which he would cross over his chest tucking the fringes in his braces. After wishing us all goodnight he would go into the shop and take out his beer money and ½ oz of Franklyn's tobacco and off he would go down to the Workmen's Club in Aberbeeg. In those days it was strictly a men's club and Dad always said, 'The day they allow a woman into that club will be the last day for me'. [EW]

Courting

When you were courting you took things slowly you didn't want to jump into bed with anybody. You'd start off holding hands and that was lovely and then you'd go quietly from there. The bands were called out for three weeks before in chapel. [RM]

After I started courting, my husband used to come and meet me from chapel and we used to go for a walk. Everybody did their courting in the pictures. There were four picture houses here in Abertillery and the Palace used to change their programme half-way through the week so you had five to go to. The queues used to be really long both first and second houses it was 10½d to go downstairs and 1/9 to go upstairs. [JL]

Blaenau Gwent Workmen's Club skittle team, winners of the Aberbeeg Hospital Cup in 1941.

Abertillery Cricket Club Ladies Committee, late 1950s.

Cinemas and Market Hall

The main entertainments we had were the cinema and dancing. We had five cinemas – the Gaiety, the Empress, the Palace, the Pavilion and the Metropole Theatre. Then there was the Market Hall for dancing on a Saturday night – sixpence for a dance – and we used to thoroughly enjoy ourselves. All that's gone now that the television has arrived... a pity. [WGH]

Of course, in town they had four cinemas and the Market Hall and the station was like Piccadilly Circus on a Saturday night or any night. And Market Street, oh dear me. They didn't have it regular but they used to have travelling theatres and they'd put a play on over a weekend. [MH]

Greyhound training

I remember old Pat Flaherty used to train his greyhounds on the flat road going across the mountain above Bishop Street. He had an old bicycle frame with a bit of rope round the back wheel and a piece of rag or rabbit's fur tied on the end. He would wind it up and the dog would chase it for about a 100 yards. The frame was up there for a number of years and lot of people used it. Old Pat used to tell the boys, 'Wind like hell!' [KB]

Formation of the Wheelers

My father bought me a second-hand bike and I learnt to ride around the back streets and in Powell Street.

Then, every Sunday, I got up, cut myself a few sandwiches and I'd be wandering around the countryside on this bike. I did that for years on my own before I met up with the Cyclists Touring Club in Cardiff and they said, 'Join us.' I'd go down and meet them outside Cardiff City Hall by nine o'clock on a Sunday morning. We'd ride around the Vale of Glamorgan and sometimes over to the Forest of Dean. I had a couple of coppers in my pocket so I could go and have a cup of tea.

Before the Second World War, we formed a club in Tredegar and I was riding there for a couple of years. Then, the war came and all the boys went to war and we had to disband it. Towards the end of the war there was a boy in Abertillery, name of Georgie Wynn, who was riding for Cwmcarn Paragon and I met him in town by the war memorial and he said, 'Why can't we form a club in Abertillery?' So, we rounded up as many boys as we could and formed Abertillery & District Wheelers in 1945. [MM]

In tandem

I had a tandem bike and my daughter would be on the back and we would ride out together on a Sunday. She got so used to it that I could have taken the back handlebars off – she never used them. We did this for years until she started courting and wanted a bike of her own. One Saturday afternoon in the summer months, when she was about four or five-year-old, we decided to go down to Barry. Of course, I knew the side roads to go on and it didn't take me very long to get down to Barry, only

Abertillery polo team, 1930. Among those pictured are Reg Hoskins (left of front row), Grail Samuels and Reg Hanney.

about an hour and a half. We spent an hour or two on the sands and I bought her a comic and a sunshade. We started back about six o'clock and I decided, instead of going back the way we'd come, I'd come back through Cardiff. 'Put that sunshade in the bag at the back', I said to her before we set off. Well, as we were coming through the main streets of Cardiff everyone was stopping and I could see them all looking. I couldn't understand what the trouble was. It was only when I come on to Newport and started going up to Forge Lane and Bassaleg that it struck me and I looked back. She'd come through Cardiff with the parasol up, reading her comic on the back. No wonder the people were staring at us! [MM]

Sport

I was interested in sport all my life. That was life, sport, football, swimming, water polo. I was brought up in it. [RH, who played in three Welsh trials at water polo]

Tillery Institute baths

They spent a lot of time in Tillery Institute and for swimming, oh 'Tricky' [Albert Williams] was clever. Reg Hoskins and 'Tricky' taught me to swim, I used to go up late in the evening when the baths were closed when they were training. My father was there as well. Also at the baths at that time was Stan Williams, who was in charge of the baths. The boys used to

Abertillery Swimming Club. Among the members are Percy and Albert Williams.

practice late in the evening for the polo team and I would go in with them sometimes and that's how they taught me to swim in the water with them. But oh 'Alb' was wonderful he'd be in the water and there was nothing he couldn't do with tricks in the water and that's how he came to be called 'Tricky'. They used to have swimming galas and 'Tricky' would always do his stint in the water and perform for everybody. They all loved him. He and Reg Hoskins would have their hands and feet tied and they could still swim the length of the baths. They did that for exhibitions. [AH]

Most of my swimming was in the Powell Tillery baths. I also swum in the Park baths and in the lido which was made by all unemployed workmen. The unemployed people down Six used to run it, they had three or four working on it. We used to go down in the night-time, when the crowd had finished there. 'Tricky' and myself used to have the baths to ourselves and we would swim back and fore for half a mile or more. Up in Tillery Baths it was thruppence or fourpence if you were a member if you belonged to the colliery. Otherwise, it was sixpence if you were an outsider using the baths. When we went down the lido I think it was tuppence. [RH]

I taught people to swim and I've had people come to the house and ask if I

Six Bells lido, built by the voluntary labour of unemployed men in the 1930s.

would teach their kiddie to swim. 'Alright.' 'What do you charge?' 'I tell you what, 10 shillings and guaranteed to teach 'em to swim whether it's a week or a twelvemonth.' I had three or four pupils like that. [RH]

Bringing up bodies

Albert [Williams] was a good trick swimmer. We lived for it, we went everywhere swimming. One day, someone fetched me to go to Penyfan. He said, 'I want you to come up Penyfan to bring a body up'. I said, 'OK, let me give my pal, Albert Williams, a shout'. I went up in Super [Superintendent of Police] Powell's cab to Penyfan Pond and there was one or two chaps there. I said, 'Where did the body go in?' They told me the mark and I went in diving. Jack Musselwhite, the superintendent of Pontllanfraith baths, was in the boat

and I was there over an hour diving. You go down and it's like daylight so far, then when you go down deep it's murky. You can't see and you got to grabble then and I was about an hour groping. In the end I said, 'Well, as far as I'm concerned, you won't find him... the only thing that'll happen is he'll come up on his own'. I was right. The next morning about eight o'clock a nurse was going that way to work in the hospital and she seen the body floating on the water. [RH]

Football

In them days we didn't have the money to go on the buses or trains. What we used to do, me and a pal of mine, Francis Trivett, Pantypwdyn, we used to walk up over the mountain and go down into the valley – they call it the Glory Hole, down over by the col-

121

Abertillery Crusaders Rugby Football Club, 1913-14 season.

lieries the Blaenserchan, Tirpentys and Llanerch and walk down into Pontypool and then we'd come out in Pontnewynydd.

We used to more or less run back up to beat the dark but so long as we got up on the mountain in daylight we was alright looking down to Abertillery, Six Bells and Aberbeeg. [RH]

I played for the school team after school, I played for the ex-schoolboys and then I played a bit for Blackwood, Brynmawr and Abertillery. I played everywhere I could get a game. In those days that was all you had, there was a lot of unemployment, and you were glad of it. [RH]

Aberbeeg RFC club song
(sung to the tune of *Farmer's Boy*)

We are the boys from Aberbeeg

The good old RFC
We train and play the season through
As happy as can be

Aberbeeg RFC, 1896-97 season, pictured outside Webbs House in Aberbeeg. In 1897 this team played Cwmcarn in the final of the Monmouthshire Cup losing by two minors to nil. From left to right, back row: John 'Abercoch' Jones (Secretary), L. Sanders, A. Crocker, G. Griffiths, -?-, -?-, -?-, E. Jones. Second row: Webb Jones, J. Boots, J. Maggs, E. Boots (Captain), G. Boots, H. Rees. Front row: H. Jones, T. Trimes, W. Hollyfield, J. Bennett, S. Carpenter.

And when we step on the rugby field
There's no-one can deny
That we play to win and we never give in
Till we've scored the winning try
Till we've scored the winning try

Of all the clubs there are in Wales
We are the one that's best
The reason is a simple one
We try harder than the rest

Repeat chorus

As long as there's a rugby field
And there's a rugby ball
There'll be a team from Aberbeeg
Ready to play them all

Repeat chorus

A hard man's game

I played rugby all my life. I played for Aberbeeg youth and for Six Bells. The baggage man for Aberbeeg threw a bucket of water over me, saying that was for playing for Six Bells so I caught hold of him and stuck his head in a bath! I got paid half a crown to go and play rugby for Six Bells. The captain was Tommy Jones; he only had one hand, the other had been cut off by a shears in work but he still managed to play well.

Six Bells rugby team, 1930s.

The team used to change under the Six Bells Hotel and walk up by the old church to play in Jack Davies' field. When we played Cwm we used to change in the hotel and walk up the Arael mountain carrying the goalpost with us. They don't know they're born today!

I used to like a singsong, after. Fred Day used to play the piano for us at the Ivorites or the Hanbury. The Ivorites could be rough at times, people from the huts and from Cwm went there. There was not a lot of fighting but people used to argue the toss. We would talk about the match on the bench outside the Hanbury Hotel. A lot of people from Brynithel played for us and a lot of Aberbeeg played for Abertillery.

When I was in my thirties I broke my fingers playing rugby. I went to pick the

ball up and I was kicked. I went to the doctor's but I got fed up of waiting. I also broke my ribs but I treated myself. I had injuries to both my knees but I wasn't going to carried off on a stretcher. [RT]

Aberbeeg rugby

We had a railway team going and we used to play in all the railway competitions what they call the All Line Cup that was played for by all the depots in the Western region. We had quite a good side then. I was only a youngster at the start and I'd be travelling as a reserve. When we disbanded, Aberbeeg rugby started up then. I am a founder member of the club. The Hanbury, that was the headquarters to

Aerial view of Abertillery Park, c. 1960.

start off with. Well one night we had a do upstairs, a social evening. This chap was there and he was as drunk as a handcart. So we put him in the car to take him home now and one of us took his car as well. But where we made the mistake was we left the ignition keys and before we could get back down the Hanbury he was there. How he used to drive I never know. I had a season up at Cwm and I had a season in Llanhilleth. The rest of the time I spent in Aberbeeg. I got made chairman and I

was chairman down there for 25 years or more, I expect. I was one of the founder members of the rugby club because we bought that off the railway as a shell. It used to be the railway canteen. We done it all out and made it what it was for many years – a good thriving club. [BF]

Abertillery Harriers, 1930.

No swearing at the rugby

Right from the time I was a youngster I was always interested in Abertillery rugby. Back in 1935, I think it was, I can remember the All Blacks playing a combined Abertillery and Cross Keys team and we went up on the Arael Mountain, up in a tree so we could look down to see the match. We used to wait till people went off the gate (that would be half-way through) and then we could go in for nothing. There was a character, they used to call him Duck and Green Peas, he had a beard and very often, I don't know whether it was his nature or whether he was drunk, but he always used to be down right up by the fence on the terracing side and he used to shout out to the players. Of course, his language wasn't all that good and in those days people didn't swear at a match. The players didn't even swear on the pitch. So, they used to catch hold of him and chuck him out. [HM]

Entrepreneurship

We had a shed at the back of the garden and you know at the top of Glandwr Street is The Park and the big rugby field. Well, when there were rugby matches there were always thousands of people that would come and the men all had bicycles. Now, the boys in the street if they had sheds they'd have cloakroom tickets and they'd stop the men with their bikes and give them half a cloakroom ticket. I can remember our shed jam-packed with bikes we'd be looking after them for these men. The boys used to put a sort of a blackboard outside the front on the road, 'LEAVE YOUR BIKE FOR A PENNY'. Then, of course, laws came in and they weren't allowed to do it. [MY]

Going north to glory

My mother's family was Rees which was quite a sporting family in the area. They all played rugby and were interested in boxing and pigeon racing. My mother's brother, David was one of the first from Abertillery to go north to play rugby league football and that happened in 1921. They called him 'Dai' Rees. He took his family up but I can't remember what the transfer fee was but it would have been a maximum of £100. Of course, there was no work around then and Abertillery didn't get back on its feet until the threat of World War II. Most of the other Rees brothers went away to work. Dai Rees played for Cross Keys and Abertillery and he went up north as a centre but as he got bigger he became a forward. He played for Halifax and toured with the 1924 Great Britain team to New Zealand. Then, in 1931 he captained Halifax at Wembley and they won the cup. Afterwards, when he got too old to play football, he managed Bradford Northern and while he was manager the club went to Wembley three times. He met royalty and I, as a kid, went up to watch and I had champagne out of the big cup. I always liked rugby league. [JL]

EPILOGUE

People these days say that people aren't as friendly as they were years ago but then people never went outside the area to work. They worked in the area, they married people from within the area and it was a very close community. Now people travel to work and when they come home they just want to be in their own homes with their families. They stay in more because they've already been out and travelled. There's ready-made entertainment in the home now. Years ago you had family living around you, you don't have that so much now. It's a different type of life. But, basically, I think people are still the same, ready to help when you are in trouble.

Everybody's better-off financially because they've got lovely homes, nice furniture, carpets, which never was before. It was coconut matting, stone floors, scrub-top tables so they are definitely better-off. But, and I expect most people would say the same, I don't think people are any happier for it. I think people were happy in those days making their own pleasures.

ACKNOWLEDGEMENTS

The following is a list of those men and women who were interviewed during the compilation of this book and without whose vivid memory and generosity, it could never have been produced. The anonymity of some interviewees has been preserved where requested but for the majority of extracts initials-based codes placed at the end will indicate the source:

The late Mrs Doris Bearcroft [DB]; Mr Don Bearcroft [DTB]; Mr Jacky Bevan [JB]; the late Mr Jack C. Bevan; the late Mr Ken Brickell [KB]; Mrs Kitty Davies [MD] and Mr Harry Davies [WGH]; Mr Keith Dykes JP [KD]; Mr Bob Fowler [BF]; Mr Douglas Harrhy [DH] and Mrs Mary Harrhy [MY]; the late Mr W. ('Billy') Hill [BH]; Mrs Beatrice Hopkins [MH]; Mr Reg Hoskins [RH]; Mrs Ada Howells [AH]; Mr Keith Jenkins [KJ]; Mrs Jean Lewis [JL]; Mr Howard Mason [HM]; Mr George Morgan [GM] and Mrs Irene ('Renee') Morgan [RM]; Mr Harry Morgan [MM]; the late Mrs Emily Newbold [EN]; the late Mr Ralph Robinson [RR]; Mr John Selway [JS]; Mr Billy 'Shilling' (Smith) [BSH]; Mr Ron Turner [RT]; Mrs Eileen Warfield [EW].

The authors would also like to thank the following who have contributed greatly to the compilation of this work:

Mrs Peggy Bearcroft ('for her limitless patience both during the compilation of this book and every day since we were married thirty-three years ago!'); Mrs Hilda Brown; Mr David Buxton; Mrs Green (Llanhilleth); Mr Bernard Jones; Huw Menai; Mr B. Pope; Mrs Jennifer Price; Mr Norman Robinson; Mr Gordon Rowlands; Keith and Irene Thomas; Mr Bill York.

Keep-fit class from Abertillery Guild Hall at Llantwit Major.